T0137500

The
Valley

In order to reach your mountaintop,
you have to go through your valley!

Isabel Hernandez

WESTBOW
PRESS
A DIVISION OF THOMAS NELSON
& ZONDERVAN

WestBow Press books may be ordered through booksellers or by contacting:

WestBow Press
A Division of Thomas Nelson & Zondervan
1663 Liberty Drive
Bloomington, IN 47403
www.westbowpress.com
1 (866) 928-1240

All Scripture quotations are taken from the King James Version.

ISBN: 978-1-9736-7949-3 (sc)
ISBN: 978-1-9736-7950-9 (hc)
ISBN: 978-1-9736-7948-6 (e)

Library of Congress Control Number: 2019918041

Print information available on the last page.

WestBow Press rev. date: 11/20/2019

A man walking on a path through The Valley.

Contents

Introduction

Your life is a story involving a variety of characters with many eventful and uneventful seasons. Some of the chapters of your story are not necessarily a reflection of who you are and yet, others are the direct result of decisions you make.

Without a doubt, you have faced, are facing or will face challenges that bring you to a place where you stop to wonder: *Where am I going?* Or, *What am I going to do?* In fact, there are moments where you probably have asked yourself: *What is going on? Why is this happening to me?*

Enjoy the experience I share of someone that begins a journey, and eventually entertains and welcomes various companions that have in reality been assigned to destroy him! This person gives a brief moment of attention to strange voices and seductive whispers to only regret it.

Enjoy the journey as each different strange voice is identified.

Caution: **These "assigned" strange voices are interested in your life as well.**

We are living in a time that everyone is looking for "answers". So much information is available to us today because of the advanced high-tech world we live in. However, there are questions that a great part of the world's population has and the answers are not easily found because so very few are willing to care for the desperate, for the depressed, for the sick, for the ones in lack.

This book brings clarity to so many important questions. *Why am I having difficulty in being successful? What is the key to financial freedom? Why am I still battling this addiction? Why am I struggling with the same problems, constantly? Why am I being kept awake so many nights with anxiety, worrying, crying or hurting so much?*

I have personally met so many people who have become very successful, yet their success has not filled them with peace or joy.

You can taste success, but not experience true peace.

You can enjoy wealth, yet not experience true joy.

So often people face death after not ever living a life of true peace, true love, true happiness, true success or understanding of what life's journey brought them through.

We were created to live life at its fullest! We are meant to make it through our valleys and to reach mountaintops, to dream big and live a great life!

We meet those who have the dreams, they work with diligence, they make many sacrifices, they cry, they fall down, they get up and continue working to reach those dreams! Then, on the other hand, we know others that sit around with envy towards the success of others.

I understand that certain life situations or obstacles just don't allow us to reach our goals or dream. However, after reading this book, you'll discover that we have been given the power and authority to succeed, and nothing is impossible!

Most success begins with a vision, a dream and mostly with great motivation. Each level of success should be celebrated. Sometimes the best way to be successful is the create a team! The team works in unity so that each member plays the role in which they are most successful.

While it is great to celebrate success, let's remember that we can only reach those happy moments through preparation. When we intentionally prepare, we are equipped to overcome challenges and obstacles. Sometimes we even face failure, but that's alright because most success doesn't just happen! The truth of the matter is, success requires focus, discipline, and intentionality!

To succeed in whatever is your vision or dream, you cannot focus on the level of difficulty required. It's necessary that you close your ears to the critics and to the many negative voices and opinions of others.

If you are passionate about something; and you are inspired to move forward towards a vision; then put your faith to walk and have no pride in asking the one who created you to help bring you to your mountaintop –your victory!

This book is about walking through a **journey** called "**life**". We learn how we can reach victory in the midst of any and all attacks from our enemies. We learn how to make our dreams a reality by activating the weapons, power and authority given to us by God.

I hope you will be inspired and strengthen with courage to dream, to see the reality of your success and to live with a perpetual dose of peace, love, joy and success!

This book will remind us not to abandon our dreams, not to lose focus of our vision, not to listen to the voices of those that cause distraction, delay and opposition for our success.

You may not be aware, but you are surrounded by enemies that work diligently to stop the plan that God has for your life.

God has a great plan for your life! You have been created for a specific purpose! There is a divine perfect plan for you to be prosperous, for you to have a future, and for you to be hopeful!

Jesus said in **John 16:33**
"I have told you these things, so that in me you may have peace. In this world you will have trouble. But take heart! I have overcome the world."

Chapter 1

My Journey – A Walk Through the Valley

I woke up this morning standing directly in front of *The Valley's* entry gate and this is not just any gate! It stands tall, wide with elegant wrought iron vertical bars completely covered in gold, creating a prosperous and dramatic sight.

Right under my feet there's a shiny cobblestone platform, creating an over-sized welcome mat with beautiful intense jade-colored grass surrounding all areas that border the cobblestone platform. The blue skies are magnificently decorated with an amazing collection of pastel-colored butterflies!

Alright now, it's time to begin my journey. But first, let inspect my shoes, one at a time. I'm sure glad that I'm wearing these lightweight, runner shoes that are comfortable in any terrain. And, I'm wear my favorite lose-fit jeans and my short-sleeve shirt made of breathable and lightweight fabric. Oh yeah, I'm ready.

I've got to wait one more minute because I almost forgot to inspect my backpack. I have some snacks, wipes, sunscreen, bug spray, water, a swiss army knife *with just a little bit of rust on it,* matches, chewing gum, a whistle, a thin wool blanket, and a couple of other things. Oh, and a **Book** a friend gave me. I don't know if I'll have time to read, but here it is anyway. Yup, I'm ready!

Just as I was getting near here, someone offered to tag-along with me, but I really prefer to cross this valley on my own. I don't want any distractions or disruptions that will cause any delay.

I begin to walk and my mind also begins to walk! I'm remembering everything that I was told just up until yesterday by some friends. I was overloaded with advice, tips and comments about what I might expect while in this valley. For a moment, I was feeling concerned, and nervous – because of the warnings I received. I'm told I'll face rough roads so I'm really not looking forward to that part of my journey, but I don't have a choice; they're part of this valley and there's a possibility that I either walk on those paths or get near them. I can't understand it but someone told me that on some of the paths, I may agonize for a moment. I don't understand what that really means but, I hope it's not true.

Others have shared their experiences with me about their journey through the valley and now that I'm thinking about it, I honestly cannot relate. Maybe one day I will.

Although I'm not quite sure what to expect, I've been told that I will be interrupted by strange voices, with unpleasant names; whatever that means. In fact, if I put too much thought into it, the description of their identities frightens me. But I can't see how this is going to affect me. I'm highly intelligent and I'm not letting anything or anyone get in my way. I've been told that these characters will introduce themselves simply by allowing me to hear their voices; kind of directly sounding in my mind. Nope, I have no idea what that means. If I think about it too much, I get nervous, so enough! Everyone thinks differently so, maybe these strange voices won't be so strange to me; and maybe they won't bother me at all.

Wow, this is a beautiful valley! From here I can see the gentle and gradual slopes of the hills. This is actually a swell road and the weather is cooperating with my start!

I've walked several miles already and I've just noticed that this road is narrowing-up. The open field to my left and to my right are no longer as wide as they were this morning. They were a far-reaching stretch on each side but for a while now they are reducing evenly on each side. I'm now approaching a thinly wooded terrain. There isn't much green here and well, I'm not feeling so great at this very moment. I'm already feeling a little weak and wonder how I'll be able to make it through to the mountaintop.

As I walk, once again, my thoughts are in fast-paced motion, remember what others shared with me before I began this journey. I don't know how much of what I was told is true but supposedly this journey includes periods of hurting and suffering.

I can't stop thinking about something that my friend told me which really doesn't make much sense but he kept repeating over and over that I should remember that sometimes we must prepare to fight; that sometimes we face battles; that sometimes we go through war seasons. And his words make me just a tiny bit uneasy...just a bit...like who doesn't like a battle? Why would anyone tell me this right before my journey? Why not say *"bon voyage"* or *"have fun"* 'huh', that's too easy I guess.... Well, I'm not sure what lies before me, but maybe it's just all a bunch of tall tales and nonsense that get people hysterical for no reason at all... let's keep walking and see what I'm in for.

Alright now, enough thinking.... time will get away from me and then it will be nightfall.

I'm so excited! I have dreams and great plans for my future! I have a vision of what I want to accomplish and getting through this valley is key! I'm so encouraged because I know I can do this!

Chapter 2

Distracted by Strange Voices

Now, what is that? Just a few feet ahead, did I see something move? It's a dreary shadow, levitating on the side of the road, just fluttering there, almost as if it's waiting for me. (*stepping up my pace, tightly pulling my bag against my back, and pulling the straps down just to fasten it a little closer to my body*). Oh, I hope that I can keep walking without becoming petrified because I'm feeling spooked!

I know what I'm going to do; I'm going to act as if I don't see anything at all and just keep walking past it. I hope this works!

I'm beginning to feel a grave wrench in the pit of my stomach.

'Eh?' A whisper blabs out from where I thought I saw a shadow:

"I am quite important and my name is **Confusion**. I will not harm you. My only intention is to accompany you. I am here to help you so that you do not get lost. I know all of the paths throughout this valley. I can be of help to you."

Without stopping my walk, and with my heart thumping a thousand beats per second and feeling as if it's about to forcefully pierce its way out of my body.... I respond: "Well, **Confusion**, I feel my head spinning as you speak to me. I feel you are not needed, and, I don't plan on walking with you. This is an important journey and I need clarity as to where I'm going. I don't want to get lost so please get away. Just stay here, okay, just stay here and I'll keep walking."

I have to really stop and think now. Maybe there is a better path to cross the valley? This journey is beginning to feel difficult to face all alone.

'*Sigh*' I am standing next to **Confusion**! Now I'm not sure as to what I should do. I feel something strange. Oh no! What is happening to me?

I feel nervous, tense, and anxious! No, I'm not at peace…. I'm scared! This is horrible and I want to feel better. I need to sit for a moment and think which is the best way to cross the valley.

Oh, my goodness! I feel confused! I can't understand how **Confusion** came across my walk but perhaps **Confusion** knows more than I know and can help me. What? What am I thinking?

I have to remember my goal is to get through this valley and I can't be interrupted. I've got to focus, I have a clear vision of where I'm going, what I want and I'm going to keep moving. I can't be confused!

Now, let me try to remember, where am I going? I am going to cross the valley. That's it! I can't forget! My heart is beating so fast that maybe I should get a bandage and strap my chest so that it doesn't pop out! I can't forget where I'm headed so, I'll walk – fast, yes!

"**Confusion**, don't get near me again. Don't bother me because each time you get too close to me, I begin to forget my plans and this can't happen again. You are not part of my plans. Thanks for offering to walk along but my thoughts get a little foggy when you're near. Stay away."

Confusion responded: "I am not trying to harm you. Let's go, follow me. I will help you cross the valley. It's easy. I have associates that will help you as well. You're going to meet them soon, along the way."

'*Sigh!*' I'm so tired. I don't feel like walking anymore. This just doesn't feel right. I need to stop for a moment, focus, and plan on what I should do. I can't afford to get lost and now I'm feeling so lost.

What happened to the beautiful clear day? It's dark and there's a dense fog out all around me. It's beginning to get '*ugh!*'… It reeks of gaseous and musty-sewerage! I wish I had someone that I can talk to. I wish this walk through this valley was over already.

The journey just began and I already feel like I'm about to faint! It's okay- I'll just keep moving. I have to make some progress. Now I'm really tired; I'm sleepy. I'm gonna sit here for a few minutes.

A faint whine mumble …."Hey there. Hi, well, hello, hi there. Yeah, It's me. I'm sad. I'm very downhearted today, well, every day I feel the same. I'm **Depression**. I'm here to accompany you on your journey. I'm a little down-spirited today, well, every day I am, but, we're a team. **Confusion** and I are a team and I just have to tell you that we're not going to leave you alone. We're going to stay with you and since we know this valley better than you, we will make it easier for you to cross it. You have no idea of how many are walking in this valley. Some turn back because they can't handle the difficult paths but others make it to the other side, to the mountaintop. Some faint, get weak, and *'kaputs', 'ziltz'*, yup, they end it all, right here, right in the middle of their journey. We have to be honest with you. This is quite a difficult walk. At times, you may want to just cry and continue to cry. You might even feel like you can no longer walk or even open your eyes, that's how weak you might get. But, I, **Depression**, I'll be your helper! I am a true friend. So, please pay close attention to us and you will be just fine. You must listen to us so that you do not take any dangerous detours. We want to make sure your trip is not prolonged. And, besides, we don't want you to feel alone, so we will stay with you. Is that fine with you? I can give you so many ideas of what you can do to end your loneliness; your sadness; if you want. Just remember, you really need me."

I can't believe this is happening to me!

"Please listen to me, **Confusion** and **Depression**! This is my plan: I need to cross this valley to reach my dreams, my success. You see, I have plans for my future and I'm not going to allow you to become an obstacle. Don't stay near me because you both make me feel, well- the truth is you both make me feel dismal. **Depression**, things are not pleasant with you near me. Each time you walk by my side, I slow down, I feel like crying, and I feel sort of, kind of, well, low-down, blue, you know…unhappy. You've made me feel like there's no purpose for my life. Just in a matter of minutes, all of these awful thoughts and feelings have taken over me! I don't feel anyone loves me or anyone misses me. It's better if you stay here and let me walk without you. Each time you get near me I feel desperation, crummy, and miserable! I really feel better walking without you. I can't walk with you!"

"Well, I'm smart. You may not like my name but it's just a name… *'argh'* **Depression**! My opinion is that if you walk alone, things will not go well for you. In fact, things may not go well for you now or ever, here nor there, yup that is the truth. Does this all make any sense to you? Well, who cares, I'm telling you, it is better if you allow us to walk with you.

We know the valley and you don't. We are experts in helping others. You have no idea where you are going. What if? What if you mistakenly take a detour and never get to where you want to? Just place your trust in us. We're going to take good care of you. If it makes you feel better, I have an idea. I think that you should walk and we follow, quietly, directly behind you. Is that fine with you?"

I can't believe that this is actually happening to me.

"No, **Depression**, no! You cannot continue to walk with me. Please stay as far away from me as possible."

I started off just fine until these two pessimistic *things, voices,* whatever they are, put a damper on everything! All the joy I was feeling is gone! I was so motivated! I was fine and then, all of a sudden, I don't know how everything changed and all I feel is hopelessness. I was fine, I was – maybe I should quit. I don't want to quit and go back; that would be cowardly; I need to cross this valley. I'm not a loser; I'm a fighter; and I can do this!

Okay, I'll concentrate and come up with a plan of how to escape from these two naysayers that are clearly nothing but affiliates of destruction!

I'm not a coward. What am I thinking? I'm not going to let anyone-or anything- or whatever order me around. I'm in charge of me!

"Don't talk to me anymore! Do you hear me? I don't want you to whisper anything else in my ears! Your susurration, your mutter, your voices need to stop – now! Get away from me because I won't let you slow me down!"

"Hey there, I know that I'm a little late, but I've been trying to reach you. The good news is that I'm here now!"

'*Ak!*' I can't believe this! Another voice?

"My name is **Sadness**. I am part of the powerful squad! The others have informed me that you are trying to cross the valley... '*Ahem!*' alone? Really? Why would you want to do this on your own? So many others have died trying to cross this valley on their own. So, if you allow us to accompany you, you will be better off. Let me explain, you most likely will not understand because our *kingdom is secretive...*, but we have an assignment. We have been ordered to walk with you! If you want to walk, we will walk. If you want to rest, we will rest. We will linger near and never leave you alone."

'*Chuckle*' "Oh really? Well, **Sadness**, the truth is that I don't need you or your other squad members. I was just fine without you all and now that you are all here, I'm having a difficult time - I'm asking you politely to please leave."

Sadness insists "You have no idea! You see, we are many! Together we form a powerful army of chaos! You are our assignment! We have no intention of getting away from you! You have to find a powerful weapon, a powerful army to fight us off because we're not leaving voluntarily. We're here to stay! In fact, we are accustomed to being accompanied by many more. Soon, you will see. So many people reject us at first but then they realize we're needed and sooner or later, accept us, and, they actually end up enjoying our company. Others don't want ties to us and somehow figure out a way to escape. I do not understand why anyone would want to do that. Why would they want to walk alone? You should take my advice. You are better off allowing us to walk with you. This is a journey consisting of many detours. The detours involve deception, enticement, allurement, pranks, pitfalls, and more. So, face it, you need us. That's it! Some get sick, some faint and other die! Don't be afraid to experience something atypical- a different environment; You should get to know us. In fact, if we walk away from you, you will soon begin to miss us. So, do you want to be alone? Loneliness is not a good thing. You may not like our company at this moment because we are rather a 'new experience' but it's better than being alone. Isn't it awful to feel lonely? We are many, ready to accompany you."

I don't understand what is happening to me. I feel so sad, and I feel weak. I wish they would stop whispering in my ears! I want to lie down, cry and feel sorry for myself. I feel like I should close my eyes in a dark room and sleep. No one understands me. I know that no one really cares about me. It's true.

Sadness does not leave me and is comfortably sitting right here, right next to me. I think **Sadness** does care about me. But, all of them, **Sadness, Depression and Confusion,** they are all making this journey difficult for me.

They are determined to stay with me. I'll just sleep for a while and when I wake, maybe they'll be gone and I'll continue to walk.

This flat rug-like mix of dried grass, hay and sandy soil looks like a good spot to rest for a few hours. I'll get my blanket out, and get comfortable. It's cool outside but my blanket is warm, and smells clean too... 'Ahhhh!' Oh goodness! I can't sleep! I'm starting to believe that I need medication to sleep. I'm going to keep that in mind for the future. If I can't get a prescription, maybe I can ask someone if they can get some for me anyway. I might have to spend a lot of money paying for it but if it helps me sleep, well, then why not? I need to feel better soon so I can keep walking. I can't stay stuck here, out in the middle of nowhere. I just have to keep telling myself that I'm not weak and I won't faint.

Alright, I've slept for a few hours, but I'm not feeling so good. When I first entered the valley, the air was clean, crisp and pleasant but as soon as I began to hear these strange voices, the stench has overwhelmed my surroundings – the smell can suffocate me! I feel like I'm living a nightmare! Somebody please, wake me up! Why do I feel powerless? I'm already tired of feeling this way. There has to be a solution.

So, the best way to do this, to get away from them - is to think of a plan and keep it a secret. So many times, when we have plans, we share them with others and then our plans are ruined. This is exactly what is happening to me. We think that if we share our plans, others will be happy for us; but the reality is, this isn't always true.

I need to stop, think, focus, I'm smart, strong, courageous and I'm going to continue to move forward. Although I don't have an escape plan yet, I am going to keep moving. This journey is part of my existence; I have to get through this; I have to think and move without sharing my plan. I can't wait to cross this valley!

Time goes by and I don't have a solution. I'm now feeling weak and these tormentors continue to follow me. As I walk, I've noticed that I feel peace for a few minutes and then they return; when they return- I can sense their presence. This is incredible – they're a burden! I don't want them around me! They're making this journey awful for me! I'm counting on them getting tired, exhausted and then maybe they'll give up and leave me alone!

It's warming up now, the temperature is rising; it's getting awfully hot out. I'm perspiring and my feet are getting kind of sweaty too. My feet feel like they're baking, and there are a lot of stones and stumbling blocks on this path. I bet they're swollen- my feet, I'm sure they're swollen. Soon I'll have to stop walking.

This path is odd, a little peculiar. The scenery has completely changed! Wow- there are acres of deciduous live oak trees on my left and acres of white crape myrtle trees on my right. As far as my eyes can see, thousands of hanging-curved branches create the gloomiest view. On my right, large clusters of white flowers decorate the tips of the branches and bright sun rays shine through them, creating a well-lit path. The contrast in this scenery can be compared to my life. Some things go well and at the same time other things don't. There's no way to control what happens in life. I'm reminded of a lot of experiences I've had. There were times when all I wanted was to laugh, play and have fun but then some awful things happened to me that totally robbed me of my childhood joy. I don't want to re-live them. I don't, I really don't, it's painful to remember.

What's going on now? Where's the sun? It's early yet and why is it getting so dark out? It's suddenly foggy too. This feeling of grief and loneliness is growing. I wish I had a friend with me right now. I wish someone would walk into my path— anybody- I just don't want to be alone. I know we're supposed to be careful about who walks with us but sometimes it's terrible to be alone. This reminds me about some time ago, about an unhealthy relationship I was in. It was something I should have walked away from, but I didn't. I knew I didn't deserve to be mistreated; I knew I didn't deserve to be mistreated and I should've walked away but the thought of being alone is powerful.

Oh great! It's sunny again so I now have visibility. Just a few moments ago, I was afraid I was going to trip and fall. The path was sandy, grainy and covered with pebbles, creating a struggle for me to continue my walk. But now, this path is smoother, making it easier to tread along.

After several hours of walking now, I'm feeling exhausted. My eyes feel heavy and they feel warm; In fact, my entire body feels achy.

There are acres of sapling pine trees that have scattered cones throughout this area with needles that are spread in bundles.

As I break for a drink of water, I stop to listen to the sounds of nature. I can hear the birds chirping, the sound of different bugs and the soft whistling of waving branches of the trees. Hmmm, I really don't think I've been able to get the strange tormentors to stop following me.

I'm beginning to get it now; I'm beginning to understand why every time I told someone that I was about to begin my journey, they all felt it was necessary to share their experiences, well, in a warning-type of manner. Now I'm beginning to get it. I couldn't understand when they would express their trials and challenges in this valley. I wasn't sympathetic because I couldn't relate to anything they were saying. I never understood what they were talking about; when they mentioned uncontrollable obstacles sent by enemies to hurt them, to confuse them, to depress them; and now, I'm beginning to understand. I didn't ask to be confused or depressed or sad but this is exactly what I feel. I can't control what I'm feeling, I just can't.

One thing I know for sure is that I don't plan on stopping here. I won't stop and stay. This hurts too much. It doesn't matter how much my feet ache, I'm going to keep walking. I'm not staying here; I've got to do something to feel better.

Alright, I'm going to get better. I'm going to avoid conversations with these strange voices, I'll ignore their whispers and I'll stay focused.

I wish someone was with me to understand what I'm going through. Of course I want to walk, to move forward, out of this valley, but I can't explain how I'm feeling right now. What am I going to do?

Sometimes my mind is not clear. Could it be that I'm in the wrong place?

It's **Confusion's** fault. It is of no help to have **Confusion** near me. My thoughts are disordered, disorganized, and that is not a good thing. I try, I really try to get my thoughts in order but it's difficult for me to do so and I think it's because **Confusion** is near me.

I have to sit now. I'll sit here. This is amazing – this large coffee-colored boulder has got to be over fifty feet tall and probably twenty-five feet wide. There are others piled up directly behind it; some darker and some in a grayish-brownish tone; some wider and taller and some smaller; but I'm sitting here for now; I'm going to place my throw blanket down right next to this one; and I'm going to sit and rest. I'm so tired. As I try to comb through my short dark hair, I notice that it's feeling a little silky-well, not exactly, it's actually feeling greasy. I bet it's looking shiny too.

I can't allow everything that is happening around me to prevent my purpose in my journey! Why is this all happening? Just when I'm given a great opportunity, some enemies decide to distract me.

Wow- I can feel their presence near me; I wish they'd stop. They're persistent, annoying, dominant and I must admit, very influential. I have thought over and over that maybe I should give in and let them walk with me.

My face feels dirty; It was humid today and the dust hovering around my feet has made its way up from the ground to cover my eyes a little; and they're irritated. Why didn't I bring a mirror? I bet my eyes are red. It doesn't matter what time of the day it is; it gets very dark sometimes in this valley. The thick dark heavy clouds are beginning to cave in and surround me. I'm beginning to get a weird feeling.

These voices are making me think I've flipped out!

Why did I open my ears to entertain "these voices"? What happened to me? I was curious, that's why! I wanted to listen to what they had to say but I didn't think that they would attach and torment me. I was warned before I began my journey. My friend warned me about entertaining for a split second or responding at all to any strange voice in the valley. But, as usual, I always think I know it all. I usually feel intelligent and self-sufficient and I realize that I need to be more humble; I should have listened!

Depression keeps getting near to weaken me. When I feel weak, I feel confused and when I feel **Confusion** I am overwhelmed with **Sadness** because I don't know what to do! I can't make decisions! I can't focus! And, I am trying to be happy but it is not happening! I think about all the things that I can do to be happy but it's not working. I have no motivation to even move from here.

It's getting dark again and I feel like running but I don't know where to go! What a terrible feeling! It's awful to feel no motivation, to feel depressed, and want to run away but to run where?

I'm going to have a snack and not think- just eat; that's it. Oh, wait, I brought my headphones with this tiny music player. I'll listen to some music…. 'nah', this music isn't improving my mood. In fact, this snack isn't helping either. I'm intentionally trying to feel better; but it isn't working.

Maybe if I say a prayer. Who knows if God will hear me talking. I'm not sure that's possible. Someone told me that I waste my time if I pray – How can there be a God that hears me? But, what if, what if there is a God and what if God can hear me? It's better to try than not to try. Oh, I don't know!

Depression causes me to cry. Last night, I couldn't stop crying because **Sadness** got comfortable next to me and it got so bad I felt as if I didn't want to live any longer.

"Come here! Stop walking so fast. I, **Depression**, I want to help you. I heard you talking to yourself and I want to hold your hand."

"No, I'll hold your hand. **Depression** has bothered you enough! You need me! You need me, I'm **Sadness**. I'll hold your hand and help you. I'm a good **Sadness**. I make you feel better after I make sure that you cry for hours."

"Neither one is as strong as I am. Let me hold your hand as I am more powerful. I am **Confusion**. That is who I am. I can hold your hand and you will not regret it. In fact, you'll forget why I'm holding your hand."

Can it be that they understand how desperate I am to be without them? I can't describe how I feel. I need help. Now I understand why sometimes others don't feel like they can continue their journey, their life plan. This isn't easy! Day in, day out; people go through life feeling like this; this is horrible. Others walk past me in this valley and they don't even notice me. It's like I'm invisible out here. I try to get their attention, but they all keep walking.

I'm in trouble now. I accepted their companionship because I did what I wasn't supposed to do. That's all they needed to begin their assignment against me. I'm thinking about the **Book**. I don't have time to read and what a strange gift to hand someone right before they're going on a journey!

This is it! I've made a decision! Although my feet are in severe misery, oh they ache and they just feel awful; and, my head feels exaggeratedly tight, like it's holding a loud and powerful thunder inside, but I need to keep walking.

Oh my goodness! Sure enough! There's another one; It's a dull, soft and annoying voice:

"It is impossible for you to ignore me as I am remarkable! My name is **Discouragement**. Where are you headed to?"

I'll just ignore this voice and maybe it'll fade- permanently!

"*Har, har,* you just can't ignore me. Let me remind you that you may be interrupted by raging and vicious creatures in this valley. Who knows? You may face lions, serpents, wolves, and more! And let me remind you of how weak you feel at this moment. What are you thinking? There is no way that you can cross this valley without me. You can be killed along the way! In fact, I bet your feet hurt, and that you are dry-thirsty, utterly-exhausted, and immensely-anxious! You need me- you need me to walk by your side. You should feel sorry for yourself. It is a terribly sad thought that you would have to cross this valley alone. Besides being alone, remember that your feet hurt! You are tired! It is unfortunate to be on a journey, not knowing how long it will take for you to arrive to your destination. What is the point? You can stop here and die. That is an idea; or, you can allow me to walk with you and the rest of our squad; or, just with me, if you'd like. But you can't go alone."

I hate to admit it but **Discouragement** is right - It's true! I'm feeling so weak. For the last few seconds, I thought of what I should respond to **Discouragement** and I practice in my mind what I should yell out to **Discouragement**, but...I'm dry-thirsty, my mouth and throat feel like cotton; and I'm lonely. Why not let **Discouragement** walk with me? What kind of harm can this cause?

I continue to stroll along my path- trying to tune out the voice of **Discouragement**.

"I know you don't know what to do. Your thoughts are shuffling and you're wondering what to do... but keep me...please keep me around... ."

"Stop talking to me! **Discouragement**, leave me alone. I'm begging you!"

Why am I feeling hopeless? I can hear a haunting ringing in my ears getting louder and louder- my eardrums might just perforate! Where did these tears come from? My eyes have filled to the brim with tears, but I'm not going to allow one to roll, nope, not one! Oh, oh- yup, yup - a water dam broke and my eyes and even my nose is dripping now!

Discouragement continues to speak without inhaling for fresh air: "I know you don't believe me, but if you don't listen to me, you'll be sorry. Soon you will see the dried bones of the others that have died on the way; you will get frightened, go back and never make it to where you want to go. Well, maybe you should give up now and go back- forget about crossing the valley if you don't want me to accompany you."

"No, I don't need you, **Discouragement!** I really don't. I'm trying to battle all of these voices that have surround me. I need to sleep and wake up to a fresh new morning and continue my journey!"

Discouragement doesn't quiet down: "Let's reason here, let's think things through very carefully. We can make it an unforgettable journey and keep the entire team together. We'll keep you company. We might have fun, well, in reality, we won't, but at least you won't be alone. What do you say to that? That's the problem, you don't want to trust us. Did someone try to turn you away from us? We're good for you! It's time that you think for yourself and stop remembering any advice anyone has ever given you against us. Think about it, if we all accompany you, you can relax. You can take naps, ignore everyone else that tries to talk to you and just rely on us. You don't need friends nor family. I feel as if someone has tried to warn you against us before you began this journey. If you ignore us, you will miss out! We will teach you new things, take you to different places and help you enjoy exciting new experiences! You are so concerned about crossing this valley but what you should do is enjoy it with us! Think about everyone in your past or anyone that wants to be a part of you. I'll tell you the truth: You are nothing special to them! If you think that you are special to anyone, then explain to me *why are you walking alone?*"

I think I'm walking on a steady incline; my backpack is getting heavy; dense-cool air has quickly moved down from the slopes into my path- it's a little breezy, just a little. I can hear crickets, screeching owls, wolf howls- and hopefully they're far away. This is not good! I'm going to take a nap for now. It's late anyway. Maybe I'll sleep all night and start walking again in the morning. Maybe they won't talk to me again.

Discouragement is right. Nobody cares about me and I am all alone. I have been lied to; cheated on; mistreated; mocked; treated horribly; and I have had a lot of losses. I have gone many nights with groans of uncontrollable crying. I will do whatever I have to, but I will cross this valley. I'm not just going to give up! Someone once told me that I have a purpose in life! I don't know what my purpose is yet- but there's a plan for me- there's a reason for my being and I need to cross this valley! And I will.

Chapter 3

Others Pursue Me

Everything surrounding me is dipped in morning dew. The birds are determined to wake up the valley with their singing- oh, and there's a family of sow-bugs and pill-bugs that are crawling just a few inches away from me! I'll scoot over a little to my left and pull my backpack with me.... What do I have to eat in my bag? These snack bags are good- and I'll walk while I eat... What an awesome view! All sorts of levels of slopes- upland, hilly and rolling- continuing for a long distance. Some slopes are crooked, others shapeless, bulky; olive, and I can see the striped rows of bright evergreen trees, and the spicy, sweet and piney scent is encompassing this entire morning!

I can hear them. I can't believe it! I was sure a new morning would bring me a fresh new start- but I can hear them again. They're determined- they're united to torment me.

What is all that noise? Are there beasts nearby? Oh goodness! I can hear sounds of strange animals- are they barbarian pigs or gargoyles?

"Did I not tell you? Do you really want me, **Discouragement**, to leave? Aren't you glad we are here with you this morning? I have wonderful news for you! One of our allies has been assigned to join us but honestly, I should take the credit for the newcomer because I've attracted **Fear**. **Fear** is here to join us and make us a stronger team! You don't understand me but this is magnificent! Now, it will be difficult for you to get rid of us! But don't worry, **Fear** is going to improve your journey. We are your companions. We are all here to stay! Face it, you are now feeling lonely, heavy-hearted, and your enthusiasm is all gone. And let me remind you that you really need us. Stop rejecting us; accept me and the others. You don't want to face the swine crossing this valley all alone. After all, they're all probably very hungry!"

I can't believe this is happening to me. "Fear, please leave. Is that? Is that? Oh, I think I can hear some lions and wolves. Please, **Fear**, please go away."

"Did I hear my name? **Fear**? Yes, **Fear** is my name. *'ahh ha ha'* Did you say lions? wolves? Try adding serpents, tigers and more! *'auahaha'* But, don't worry, I am near to help you. If you decide to walk alone, you might as well run for your life because the beasts will eat you up! They're going to kill you. You're going to die! Doesn't that fill you with **Fear**? *'mwahaha'* You should sit down right now and tremble and die! Or, you can just let me sit next to you forever and live with me while you tremble. What do you think? My first suggestion? My second suggestion? *'mwahaha'*."

"What is your problem **Fear**? You're making me tremble! I feel terror, panic, horror and it's bad enough that I hear the sounds of the wolves and lions but you are devastating me!"

These losers have transformed the morning fresh air into a sour, fermented and curdled whiff! Could it be possible that I'm able to move forward without being noticed by the wild animals? I need to at least try...!

Maybe I don't have it in me to make it on my own. I thought I was smart, bold and had the strength to cross this valley but as much as I'm trying, they won't leave. **Confusion** is persistently clinging on to me; **Depression** and **Sadness** are hugging me; **Fear** is sedentary on my shoulders; and I am too weak to do anything about it!

Individually or as a clan, they're stronger than I am. Sure, I can throw a tantrum, but they're here- they won't leave. Which way should I go? What if I get lost on the way?

My walk is staggering on this bumpy-choppy path as I fight these complicated thoughts that have interrupted my focus.

The squawk and chime of an entourage of large oily palmetto bugs have determined to follow me today. I'm definitely not alone.

This area is surrounded with dead and fallen trees, with earthy rotting wood scents. The dried up logs are covered with decayed animals- that look like *'eek!'* mice and birds. The path is disturbed by slapping branches, knobby roots under my feet and I can feel spider web strands on my skin as I walk . '*oi!*' Strange not to hear the birds chirping but I can surely hear constant rustle of animals and insects humming while they rest on the faded brown twigs. I stop to lean on a rough-barked tree and lift my head up just a little, with my eyes closed. I can savor the stale, acidic and bitter wild mushroom. '*Whoosh*' The sudden strong winds have caused the tree branches to lash and crash with falling squirrels that chatter for help while they fall on a shady carpet of scratchy and dried up pine needles and pine cones.

I've lost all interest. Is this journey worth my try? My motivation is completely crippled and I feel worthless. I can feel my heart rate wildly pulsating. Should I stop? Should I forget this journey? I can put an end to everything right now, right here. I can't imagine how things will improve. I really should just put an end to my journey. I know a couple of people that couldn't cross the valley- and they did just that. Well, I now remember that a long time ago, a friend of mine made mention of wanting to stop his journey and that **Depression** had him just about convinced to do so; *and* that no one would miss him. My friend just kept moving, kept walking and although he said it wasn't easy, that he struggled, he struggled for days, months and it even went for a few years but he made it. In fact, it was just halfway through his journey that he met someone; he married her; and then they had a couple of beautiful children. They began a great successful business and oh was he darn happy that he had ignored his roommate at that time: his roommate **Depression**. He did tell me that although it wasn't easy, he got some help and was finally able to remove **Depression** from his surroundings.

All this thinking and I just realized I've covered a lot of ground. I can tell that I'm near the end of this path and I feel as if I've been marching in haste through a dark tunnel for miles. But now I can see the portal of this tunnel, '*cause* I see a bright light ahead through the oversized arch that is allowing a massive beam of sunlight to point directly at me – it's the end of this path; the end of this forested zone and the opening to....

'*Ohhh*' Fascinating nature! – What an incredible transformation in this setting. I'm greeted by verdant stunning slopes with shimmering streams of water running downwards. The shades of vibrant green moss and grass; an elevated sky that just exalts nature.... I think I'm going to sit right here next to this stream and wash my face. '*Haahh*' I'm finally able to get rid of my thirst; cool water - ahhh! I'm not sure what kind of birds they are- but they're soaring near and far; eloquently gliding- the perfectly blue sky is filled with their movements; I can't believe it but I think I'm actually smiling! Nature is just darn good-looking!

What was that? What did I just hear? *'Ugh!'* *'Nah'* It can't be.... Oh no! I thought I was safe in this area of the valley; it's clear and sunny.... I thought *'ugh!'*

'Ahem!' I'm here too. I am **Anguish**. I've arrived a little late. I don't have time to waste; I've been assigned to join this party! So, you think you can cross this valley on your own? I should remind you that you will experience a lot of hurt and **Anguish** throughout this journey. You will be hurt so much that your heart will be broken, and maybe it's even going to melt like worthless wax. Honestly, I don't understand why you just don't give up! Haven't you heard about all the suffering you will experience? Why are you so motivated to continue your journey? What is your point? You should end this now. Do you think your existence is of any importance? You're just another being, walking, but not important at all. Haven't you heard about all of the obstacles you will encounter? Just finish it all, now. No one will miss you! Life goes on for everyone else and after a while, no one will even remember you. Can't you tell that I'm telling you the truth? Afterall, look at how many other people walk past you and don't even notice you. No one cares what you've been through or what you'll face in your future."

I feel intense throbbing aches in my burned-out feet and all of a sudden it doesn't seem so sunny anymore. Maybe I should, maybe I just should put an end to this journey. I should end this season of survival. Why shouldn't I?

I wonder how many people go through what I'm going through today. Does this happen to anyone?...*to everyone?*

Who would have known that all of them: **Anguish, Depression, Sadness, Discouragement, Confusion and Fear**, would come after me, pursue me; *why me?* They're sneaky and I don't know how to extinguish them! Their voices... *murmur, whine, shriek, snort...* resounding in my ears. **Anguish** diminishes any motivation I have; I'm down right downcast with **Depression** and **Sadness**; **Discouragement** has caved-in on me and thanks to **Fear**, I'm dreading encounters with ferocious wild beasts! And, to make this even worse, I'm baffled, puzzled and filled with **Confusion** at this moment.

I really need to brainstorm and write out a plan on how I'll avoid the paths of where the fierce animals roam. I'll rest for now, regain strength and figure out a way to escape from them.

"We have news for you! I, **Fear**, will speak for all of us. I'll be very clear with you. We were sent to follow you; we have an assignment and therefore, we will stay with you as long as we possibly can. As long as you can't figure out a way to fight us off, we'll be showing up every once in a while. We gain strength when we are united and that is our mission: together we are determined to make you our permanent shelter. There are more of us, many, hundreds, thousands, but thus far, only a few of us have been designated to accompany you. It would be easier for you if you just accept us. After a while you will get used to us. Sure, sometimes you won't like us, but at other times, you won't mind having company."

I'm trying to act as if they're not bothering me. I'll sit here for a few minutes and wipe off my shoes. They're not as tidy as they were when I began my journey. Those voices; *buzz, babble, hum, jabber*; they just don't stop. They can't understand that their constant harassment has caused me to stumble over these sharp stones and my feet are severely injured. They act as if they don't care because they keep hurting me. Why can't this journey be easier? It seems like everyone else crosses this valley with smiles and giggles. So why do I have to feel so down in the dumps?

What do they mean about having an assignment? What assignment? Who has sent them? They feel they are few? Oh goodness! They are enough! I don't want any more of their helpers to join me so let me walk as fast as I can. This **Book** in my backpack – it's getting a little heavy to carry around. Maybe I should get rid of it. I better not, after all, it was a gift. I'll just keep it.

"Hey, why are you walking so fast? Where are you going? Are you planning on getting rid of me? You need me, **Confusion**, to direct you in the right path."

"You need me too. I'm so special, I'm **Depression**, I'm quiet and subtle and '*ah*' I just love to cuddle with you."

"Oh, don't forget me, **Sadness**, I'm following right along with the others."

"And you can't live without me. I watch you cry each night and make sure you wake up with swollen eyes. I'm **Anguish**, and that's my assignment. Even if it's just to remind you to wipe your tears, but you need me"

I close my eyes as if that's going to stop these voices. Instead, their voices are sharper and louder.

"**Fear** is my name! You need me to remind you that you cannot live without me; that you really can't move forward towards your goals; I'm here to protect you; I'll convince you to sit and not get anything done. Just sit. Be fearful of everything. Just sit. Be idle. You need me and my fearful game."

"Well, and not because my name is **Discouragement**, but I will remind you that no one cares about you so you better keep us so that you aren't lonely. You aren't so smart, nor special, so you can't get far without us."

"Besides, if you try to get rid of us, you will be devoured by the wild beasts that are roaming ahead of this valley. If you **Fear** that you can't fight them, <u>then stay here with us:</u>

Discouragement is willing to keep you company. It's better to be surrounded with **Discouragement's** pessimism than to be alone;

Confusion will sing a tune of complexity and turmoil so that you become disoriented. It's better to be disoriented than to walk towards your goals, your visions and dreams and then be disappointed if you don't succeed; and

You definitely need **Depression** and **Sadness** because if you have not yet, soon you will realize that no one cares about you but us! Accept us!

Accept all of us! If you'd like, we can call on some backup to join us. This is what I, **Anguish**, the smartest one of this team says, keep us, keep us and you'll have some grief, not much, well, maybe some episodes of torment... well, just keep us."

"**Fear** is my name and that I must tell you the truth; you see, you allowed just a slight gap so that we were able to join you. Do you remember your first day in the valley? You were curious and responded to our whispers. You allowed us to become part of your walk the moment that occurred. So, we are here to stay until you figure out how to get rid of us."

This is incredible! I made a huge mistake! I allowed these deadbeats into my life! I was curious but now I wish they would all leave and go back to where they came from!

It was a vulnerable moment. I embraced the first and then, that one attracted another and so on! I was lonely! Even before I began my journey, most of my friends were too busy for me. For a long time now, they all seem to be so happy in their own busy lives so I decided it was okay to chat with one of these losers! I felt sorry for myself because I felt abandoned by everyone. Now, I'm suffering the consequences!

That's all it took! I entertained the utter of one strange voice in my life and now there are several.

I have a lot of plans. I have so much I want to live for. I wrote out a list of things I want to do, places I want to visit and I have goals! I want to be a part of someone special and I want so much in life! I need to remember all that I want, and figure out my purpose and, and, well, maybe I'll say a little prayer. Who knows, maybe it'll work. I surely hope no others are assigned to accompany me. If so, I don't know how I'll be able to get through this valley.

Chapter 4

Confronting the Opposition

Today, I plan on picking up my pace and hopefully getting a little further through my journey.

'*Whewf*', it's hot today! I can feel warm drips of sweat rolling down from my head, around my hair line and down my face, around my ears and neck. I feel like I'm dressed in an oven mitt freshly taken out of an overheated oven. It's so hot out that I feel like I'm inhaling the heat that is directly above the upper deck rack of a grill, with no food on it, of course. I'm not even hungry. Lately, I have no appetite.

I've been walking for some time now and I think I lost them. Good, I hope so because their presence ruins everything! They stink, their voices are repugnant and they drain me! They can't stand to see me at peace! I usually begin each day on a hopeful note and then, out of nowhere, they show up to make sure I end the day with disappointment.

I try not to remember the things that affect my hike. I can't afford to walk any slower but I've realized that when I'm alone, I tend to think a lot. And, I'm thinking of all the mistakes I've made in the past. I've really goofed up a lot. My life would be better if I hadn't made so many wrong choices and I would be further ahead in every area of life if I hadn't made so many mistakes.

Oh, gee, what's that noise? It sounds like a buzzing air conditioner is hanging directly behind my head! The muffled sound has been humming for some time but now, it sounds as if it's very close behind me!

"Who are you? Where did you come from?"

"Hello, hello, here I am! Aren't you glad I showed up? Don't you remember me? I have visited you in the past; My name is **Guilt**. You must have forgotten me and I don't know how because I like to make a lasting impression!"

"Nope! I don't remember you and I'm not interested in your company. There's no reason to remember you. Life goes on, intruder, so you can move along away from me. Go ahead, move north, south, east or west, anywhere but move on, get away from me!"

I've got to speed up a little. No one is going to obligate me to walk with **Guilt**. We've all made mistakes, we have all made poor decisions but there's no reason for me to carry this squatter on my shoulder during my journey.

This path has an entirely different ambience than the others I've covered. There's absolutely no greenery here; dirty clay and dirty yellow, all over, no green. I can hear my own steps; and there's an awkward silence. While the path is flat, it's all dry cracked land. I have an arid taste of dust-covered crushed crackers in my mouth. The cutting wind is only causing my lips to feel dehydrated. I'm parched!

"Look at you! Your walk – it has an urgent and determined attitude! Where do you think you are going?"

"Listen to me, **Guilt**, nevermind..."

"Well- *hehehe* - This is getting even better! We have a new partner! Well, well, look who has joined us. It is the magnificent **Temptation**! Hey, how are you doing? We haven't been assigned to work together for some time now. It is great to work with you on this assignment. But this one here thinks he's going to continue his walk without our company. We most definitely need your help."

With a provocative soothing-calming voice, **Temptation** gets draws near.... "I'm an expert at helping many achieve great opportunities that no one else can. Please trust me. My goal is to entice you, attract you, encourage you to be drawn to all sorts of entertainment and enjoyment during your journey. Let's face it, you already have an idea of what this journey is all about and you're for sure going to face some awful moments so you're going to need me to make those moments a little more pleasurable. You need to keep me near; you'll be totally fascinated with me because only I can help you enjoy countless unforgettable experiences;

And, I keep my promises. I can help relieve your pain, and make sure that you are never ever lonely!"

Temptation whispered to me in an appealing, seductive and fancy manner that I, in some way, admire. Well, maybe it's not such a bad idea to have company. A change of environment may make this journey a little easier. Wow, **Temptation** has a defined personality. This voice is pleasurable.

"Darling!, Let me introduce you to my partner, **Pride**. **Pride** is smashing and extraordinary! If you allow **Pride** to walk with us, everyone will respect you. **Pride** builds up your character. You will be empowered with overconfidence and self-love. And, here's more help... **Vanity**! Everyone needs **Vanity**! **Vanity** is our show-off trophy!"

"Yes, yes, you really need us. You'll never need anyone near because we'll encourage you to feel better than others; because you are, you really are! You should walk around with arrogance and self-worship, because you are great! We'll remind you that you don't have to like anyone, and you can walk past everyone with self-admiration. If you allow us to walk with you, you'll strive for more so you become successful! I'm **Vanity**, I'm your key to obtaining anything you want! Sure, there may be times when you might have to do something not so legitimate, but the point is that you will have more than anyone else you know! Whatever you want, you can be wealthier than you've ever dreamed of, but you need me to push you to that level."

These voices, I must say, sound glamourous. They may be helpful, maybe I should keep them around.

"Alright, for a moment there you had me, but I don't need anything. I don't need you **Vanity**. I admit, your offers are somewhat enticing but I'm not interested. You can all stay here. Thank you but no thank you. You might be able to convince someone else but not me, I'm not interested in your company."

"Well, I'll speak on behalf of the rest of us; after all, you can't deny that my voice is inviting and pleasant, for that's my name, **Temptation**. May I add that I am charming, and desirable! Ok, so we'll just follow along a few steps behind you just in case you change your mind. If you do, all you have to do is let us know and we'll be here, at your service, instantly."

I'll keep moving. That's all I'll do. They don't even deserve my response. I need to keep walking.

I can hear the rustling of rough sandpaper as if someone is dragging it on the ground. If I'm not mistaken, I think another one of their helpers has caught up with us. I have a feeling that I'm about to be introduced to yet another one! Of course, I'm right! I can tell, I sense a malicious fog draping over me.

There goes **Temptation** complaining "What took you so long to get here? I almost forgot that you are also assigned to this mission."

"Can you slow down some? Don't you care to meet me? I'm **Envy**. I treat everyone so well that I'm welcomed everywhere, in all walks of life.... I'm sure you'll keep me with you at some point during the journey. I have a unique task, a challenging one. I encourage you to want what others have! Is that amazing or what? I'm a great help. Others that allow me to hang around reach for higher grounds because once they see someone else succeed, they want to do better, and I help! You need me! Aren't you glad that I showed-up? Sure, it may involve some malice, rivalry, coveting, resentment and sometimes hatred but I am great! My name is **Envy**, and I can be your best friend."

"No **Envy**, really, I'm not needing any of your help. You all don't waste any time! You all communicate with each other so fast and in a flash your team is increased with additions coming out of nowhere from here and there!"

I feel like my head is being tightened up as if a wrench has been wrapped around my forehead forcing my skin against my skull. Oh, my ears feel as if they're about to burst! I feel like screaming!

"Look, all of you, pay close attention to what I'm about to say. I am tired of all of your voices. Some of you sound as if you have a *congo* tribe playing in the background, and you all have a foul idle stench and I am now, now, well, now I'm desperate for you all to disappear! I've been patient. In fact, I've been feeling weak and acting like a coward, allowing you all to bully me. But I'm done! I'm done with you all!"

"There you have it! That's exactly why I'm here!"

"*And who are you?*"

"**Contention**. I'm **Contention**. I like you! You're sounding like me now! You are definitely going to need me. I never let anyone else win an argument. Whatever I say, I make it clear that I will not surrender, I will not quit, because I'm right. *'hehehehe'* I enjoy listening to you argue! I will make sure everyone understands that you are full of conflict, strife, discord and no one, but no one will bother you as long as I'm with you."

I can't believe that I'm having to fight off these voices. I feel frustrated but I'm not letting them get the best of me. *'Nahhhh'*, I'm not worried about any wild creatures or beasts in this valley. If others have crossed this valley, and I don't know how they have, then, I can too. I'm going to face up to these strange voices and I'm going to win! They have to disappear!

"**Contention**, I'm not particularly loving your ways; and I'm not anything like you and I'm not interested in being like you. I'm not going to need you. I've met a lot of people like you in the past and I am not about **Contention** at all."

Contention laughed with a bouncing echo that sounded like something out of a horror midnight show and snorted for a scoop of air in a choke-like manner and continued... "You don't understand, I don't walk alone; for we are many. You may not perceive them but the creatures that you may face will and they will be afraid to come near you as long as we surround you. I guess you've never witnessed it but when a wild beast sees me, it swiftly draws away and turns around as quickly as possible because it's frightened by me and the rest of us. We frighten off all creatures; dogs, pigs, wolves, you name it, they're afraid of us! It is a sight!"

Contention doesn't stop; repeating the same thing.

And while **Contention** tries to get another word in... "You are...."

"I know, **Contention** you're going to tell me how much I need you for this journey. Your friends all have the same pattern, same vocabulary, and I know your routine speech. You must work for the same boss and you are all trained in the same manner. And, well, I'll do the same and repeat the same thing to you that I've told your companions... I don't need you, so, get away from me."

I'm getting bolder; yup. I'm no coward! I'm responding to these losers but I'm walking. I may be walking slower than I'd like, but I'm moving. This backpack feels heavy. I keep thinking that I should have gotten rid of that **Book** my friend gave me and perhaps my bag would be easier to carry. I keep thinking about all that I'm going through and even if I attempt to tell anyone, I really don't think anyone will understand me.

Only because I'm experiencing all of this, I believe it myself. Because, if anyone would even try to describe that they are going through, what I'm going through, I don't think I would understand them. Am I even making any sense to myself?

"I don't know which one of you is listening, or if your entire troop, army, flock, whatever you are, is listening to me.... I'm not interested in meeting any more of you. This is so absurd! The fact that I'm even responding to any of you is making me feel like I'm insane. The only thing I've accomplished by listening to you all is that I'm behind schedule! I should be further ahead by now! Before I began my journey, I had a great plan. I had my thoughts and vision well thought out. Your distractions are so disruptive - I've lost valuable time. You should be named the *Army of Disturbance, Agitation and Torment*."

After a couple of hours of nothing but silence, just when I thought I had been successful in frightening them away; I begin to hear a soft soothing voice whispering in my ear, it had a charming tone... "I forgot to tell you something..." *'Oh'* I know that voice, it's **Temptation**. I don't know why but I'm comforted by that voice...

"**Temptation**, as much as I'm captivated by your voice, I can't welcome it anymore."

"Oh dear, it's too late, here is my help, **Curse**! **Curse** is powerful!"

"That's me alright, **Curse**! I won't hurt you, I'm just another friend that you can call on for help at any time throughout your journey. I will cause calamity, disaster, diseases, whatever you want, I can cause. Think about it, you can select which one of us you need, at any time, we're all here for you. Remember, we've been given you as our assignment, we have as much time as you need. Think about how many friends have ignored you, and what about the family members that have hurt you, *oh*, and don't forget those that you have loved so much and didn't appreciate you. We're not like they are; we're here for you, for as long as you allow us to be with you. We will never abandon you. As long as you welcome us, we are here to stay."

"Oh dear, you might be a little uneasy with the others but, I get the feeling you are comfortable with me... do you want to die alone on this journey? I can help keep you happy and entertained in this valley and trust me, trust **Temptation**, you need me, you really need all of us."

I can't, I just can't understand why I'm so mesmerized by the voice of **Temptation.**

"Aha! I knew it! I can sense that you really don't mind having us around, you have cold feet, but just trust me. Face it, you do like me and you do trust me. My name is **Temptation** for a reason.... I'm charming, attractive, fascinating, and just overly irresistible! *Ahhhhhhhh* I sure am"

"No, **Temptation,** *you* don't understand who I am! You all want me to have some kind of standoffish attitude; to become alienated from others; to become unfriendly and cold; in either a vindictive, bitter or safeguarding mode. Well, I know that I've been hurt but so has everyone else I know. I can dwell on all adversity in my past or present; or, I can be resilient, courageous, and move forward towards staying on track."

I feel somewhat agitated at the moment; walking while talking to this soul-wanderer. The road has vastly widened and I have gained a sense of vulnerability and feel very much unprotected. But I'm not telling a *soul!*

Colossal dark and sharply chiseled mountains surround me. This road has brought about a challenging and defying attitude upon me. Although I hear the voices of these spiritual invaders, there is a quietness about this valley right now. I'm going to figure out a way to fight them off.

"**Guilt,** nobody's perfect; we've all made mistakes and I'm already sorry for my past mistakes, and my poor choices. I don't need you to remind me of anything."

Anguish is clinching on to me and I'm sure of it because I'm feeling miserable and sorrowful. *Now, I've gotten to some thinking...* I just can't believe all the poor choices and decisions I've made in the past. I've paid a price though; I've suffered the consequences; I just can't believe all I've gone through. It's as if I can hear a loud train traveling at the speed of a powerful torpedo with a siren that can be heard louder and louder.... *with these thoughts!* These thoughts are making me agonize!

In fact, I think **Anguish** has played some type of sneaky trick and has taken over my feelings. I need to stop walking, I can't, I can't go on... and maybe I need to rest for a while. I'm exhausted. I've got this sick feeling in my stomach; Maybe it's time for me to sit down so I'm going to stop here for now. Why did I do so many terrible things in my past? Why? Oh! Why do I feel like this? If only I could ask everyone to forgive me! If only I had never made so many awful mistakes!

While I'm resting here, I can't believe what I'm hearing! These voices are actually comforting me! I can hear them all telling me to rest, that they'll accompany me, that they'll help me.

"Don't worry, I'm **Guilt**, I'm not going to allow you to walk alone, I'll stay with you as long as you allow me to."

"I feel the same way. You'll be so grateful with me, as I'm a special **Confusion**. I can be a great and interesting life companion!"

I don't even have the energy to respond. I can't believe how they are convinced that their ailing and powerful evilness is something that I want with me!

These days have been awful. Each day I feel weaker and just when I feel I'm making some progress, I begin to hear these voices and then I get a sick feeling inside my gut.

What is the point of my journey if I'm going to experience these awful moments? I don't understand! I just don't get it!

"Hey, Hey- Wake up! I'm here for you! You are going to laugh today because I'm in charge of you today! I have so many great ideas! I'm going to teach you about some changes you need to make, that's all, small changes, one at a time, and that's it, you won't feel grieved any longer... you'll see! I don't know why my name is **Temptation** because I should truly be named *fun*! 'Hehehehe'. You'll never find such an adventurous partner with such an amazing imagination! 'Ahhhhh'...just wait and see! Give me a chance because I'm full of fun! Life is too short so you have to live for today! Do you want to cross this valley or not? Let's make this a journey with lots of diversion - oh come on! Let's have a little fun! Don't worry, I keep secrets! I'll never let anyone know what you do for enjoyment - it'll be between you and me, between you and **Temptation**! Oh, and well, I didn't want to say anything, but you're forcing me to be honest. I'll remind you that you're not so innocent. Remember all of the lies you've told? What about all of the bad thoughts you've entertained? What about all of those times when you weren't so honest with your friends, family, and co-workers? I was there each time! You didn't notice me but my manifestation was there encouraging you and enjoying every moment!"

"Stop **Temptation**, stop! I admit, I've made mistakes but that's the old me. I'm different now. I've changed. How is it that you know so much about me?"

"I was assigned to follow you a long time ago - It was easy, in the past, to encourage you to do terrible things but lately, you've changed. You allowed me to manifest myself many times in your life. But now you're making my assignment almost impossible. My superior is furious because my skills are not working much with you."

"Let's discuss something. I'm essential! As **Pride**, I help you forget anything you've done wrong, without any remorse, without apologizing, without being sorry and in fact, I'll make sure that you won't care who is hurting, as long as you are fine. Remember that you are more important than anyone else. I'll teach you how to walk without asking anyone for help and you most certainly, you should not help anyone else either!"

"Don't leave me behind! You should want to have everything better than everyone else, because that's my name, **Vanity**, and I know exactly what I'm talking about. You are intelligent, bold, attractive and you deserve to have it all, to have the best, you do!"

"I, **Temptation**, can honestly say that **Vanity** and **Pride** are an amazing team! Just listen to them... can't you tell that they are giving you great advice? My applause to my partners! I would listen to them if I were you."

Well, for a split second I was convinced. It would be nice to have nice material things; it would be nice to have the best of everything but that isn't my goal. And here I go again! I'm listening to these voices. Although all of that is true, that it would be great to have wealth, to have the best of the best of everything, to feel on top of the world... But, I'm just desperate to cross this valley. I know where I have to go and I know what I'm supposed to do... and I'm on my way... and here I go.

"Not because my name is **Fear** but I'm afraid for you. Listen to them! You need help. I'm trembling but pretty soon it will be you! **Vanity** and **Pride** are right. If you have nice things and walk like you are the king of the world, no one will ever bother you."

"'Whooo...woooo..hoooo..' don't leave me behind! You just can't keep walking without me. You've got to understand how important I am; I'm *everlasting* important; I'm important to you, to your *future* children and *their* children; just as I was for your parents, grandparents, and ancestors. I follow families around for generations. My name is **Curse**, remember? So, that means that I can curse anything and anyone that comes near you! Or you! Did I say curse you? Yeah, I can do that too, but, if you enjoy having me around, then I'll protect you always because my powers have lasting and great authority."

That's fine, they can keep whispering in my ears and I'll walk and think; I've got to think of a way to escape from them, all of them.

Chapter 5

"Almost" Trapped by Temptation

Oh well, here comes **Temptation** again:

"Don't ignore me because I'm trying to make you realize how you can be happy. Your friends are no longer really interested in being with you, correct? Don't you realize that because you've changed so much, they have abandoned you. You have to live a little on the exciting side, take risks! Have fun! Oh, and I know you've been hurt, but that's ok,... just listen to me. '*whewf*'...you are a challenge!"

"What do you mean, **Temptation**?"

"Well, we, you know, me, **Vanity, Fear, Curse**, all of us.... we sometimes travel together, we sometimes travel with others from our kingdom, but we are always on assignment. And, well, we're pretty good at convincing others that we're needed. But you; you are stubborn! We can't understand why you don't want us to accompany you. If you are so lonely, if you are hurting so much, if you have experienced so much suffering...try something different! Allow us to help you. Please? And, not to make you feel worse than you already feel, but, I know that you have been mocked as well; often; and, ….."

"Yeah..yes, **Temptation**, I hate to bring those awful moments to memory, but you're right. I have been rejected even by my closest family members, and by the people I have loved the most. I trusted them, all of them. It hurts to remember. If you know so much about me, then you probably also know that I have been mistreated in different ways; and some have made up lies about me. But listen to me, I've already forgiven every one of them. Really, I really have forgiven them, all of them."

"I know you have forgiven them but you simply cannot forget everything they all did to hurt you. You must remember, keep it all in your mind, yes, all fresh in your mind, all of those awful things. Remember how you wanted to die? Remember how you cried yourself to sleep for months? Why should you forgive? They don't deserve to be forgiven. They should hurt like you did. It's time they get a taste of their own medicine. Maybe, just maybe, they will understand how you felt."

"Well, **Temptation**, I really don't understand what you all can do for me. How can any of you help me?"

"*Well*, there's just so much...."

...and the voice of temptation continues as a soft fading echo...

It's that voice, **Temptation's** voice, I like it... it really brings me comfort.

"I can introduce you to a world of joy! Just let me walk with you. We will guide you to success, great adventures, unforgettable joy, promotions, we will guide you to places you've never dreamed of visiting and we'll help you gain wealth, success and everyone that knows you will envy you! We can attract others to you if you'd like, you'll be surrounded by great friends, you will have everything you want. You just need to make some changes.... just some changes... you just have to say "yes", agree to allow our manifestations in your life and you won't regret it! But hurry! You're missing out on so much!"

"I'm really loving your voice, **Temptation**. Just let me think things over tonight. It's getting late, I'm sleepy and I'll let you know my decision in the morning, okay? Your proposal sounds interesting and besides, I just realized something… you do entertain me. Thank you for talking to me, you're making this journey a little easier."

If only I could keep the voice of **Temptation** near by, because the others... 'hoooo' ' whoooo'.. With **Depression**, all I feel is **Anguish**. And, I can't stand to have **Confusion** around because I feel so mixed up. Oh 'awwwhhhhauuuu' I'm yawning because I'm overly tired. Yeah, let me sleep for a few hours now and in the morning I'll feel better. Everything **Temptation** says sounds good, but... I wonder what the real deal is... after all, you don't get anything without the exchange of something.

I'll place my blanket here on this cool and shady spot. Well, and here I go again; I'm tossing and turning because I can't sleep. I keep thinking about everything I hear from these strange voices and ...well maybe something is going to happen to me during this journey and **Temptation** is trying to avoid my death! *'Awwwhhhh'* I don't know. But I can see it! I would love to have a great big house with a personal chef! And, money, and... Money takes care of a lot of problems! I'm not in love with money but yes.... I can sure use a lot of it, and now! Who hasn't fantasized about having no financial problems?

Temptation is offering me an awful lot. It's a proposal that's difficult to reject... I think I'm going to say 'yes'. After all, no one has ever offered me such a great opportunity. This may be my once-in-a-lifetime chance to have it all... to have success!

What in the world am I thinking of? I'm a good person! I can't hold grudges and be that kind of person... why am I entertaining all of these other thoughts in my mind? I can't fall into the trap of **Temptation**. I'm on a mission. I have to cross this valley *'Aaaaffffffhhhhhh'* I'm so sleepy.

Several hours later...A chorus of happy birds are singing... it's definitely dawn! I can see the changes in the color of the hills that surround me. There's an entirely different *view-scape* here... could it be that I'm almost where I'm supposed to be? The spiky grass straws are greener! I'm feeling different this morning; the sick feeling in my stomach is gone and, in fact, I'm getting so emotional; after struggling so much on my own, I think I've made progress and I'm near the mountaintop!

"Good morning my dear! I hope you slept well. I'm sure you've made up your mind... I'm offering you a whole lot!"

Wow! It's a good thing that I rested because this voice, **Temptation's** voice, is so convincing; but, I'm now thinking with a fresh and clear mindset! Of course I can't do all of those things and change to be a person full of **Pride**, **Vanity** and greed!

"**Temptation**, I didn't sleep well, I did put a lot of thought in all you're offering, and... but, my question to you is... What do you want from me in return for wealth, fame, success including everything else you're offering me?"

"Nothing my dear, I ask nothing of you... just for you to follow my advice.... follow my instructions...and...to allow me and the others to manifest ourselves in your life. Once you agree, we own your soul, well, your soul will be part of our kingdom."

"No thanks! I'm glad I had a chance to rest because now I'm thinking clearly. I must have been exhausted and feeling sorry for myself last night. I was feeling convinced by your enticing proposal."

"*'Ha!'* you think you're going to be fine walking alone? This is one scary valley...not because my name is **Fear** but you should feel terrified to walk alone! What if things don't go well for you?"

"You all may not understand me but I woke up with a refreshed mindset! Life takes courage to do the right thing. You have all come to delay my progress, you all want to make sure I don't reach my dreams, and to interfere the good plans I have. I must say, you all deserve an award for your efforts but it *ain't* working with me!"

All of a sudden, I'm getting a sick feeling in my stomach again. *'agggghhhhh' 'ohhhh' 'noooo'* I hope it's not what I'm thinking...

"I've been waiting for you."

Who is that? It's a *sharp squeaky* voice... Can it be true? It can't be! Not another one!

"Greetings! I'm **Bitterness** and I'm here to walk the rest of the way with you. Haven't you been warned about the serpents, lions and gory beasts that you might face here? You will be glad that I'm with you. You're not experienced in this valley but I am and I've been around since soon after the creation of mankind."

I can almost taste the atmosphere! It's like sipping on some vinegar-tart-flavored mouthwash! *Yuk*!

"*'Awww'* I see the acidic look on your face. You can relax... I understand that I do have some type of pungent effect on people, but I'll have the same effect on anything and anyone that comes near you, to bother you of course.... and then you'll be left alone. Did I say alone?"

"Are you kidding? I've got to keep on moving and what I need is help, but good help, and not some sour slap breath striking across the bottom of my stomach!"

That voice! **Bitterness'** voice is brutal, intense, almost offensive, and really causes a stinging and unpleasant sense in my insides!

"Fine, you think you don't need me but there will be times when you will wish that I, **Bitterness,** am with you! You'll see, when you meet fake friends, you'll wish I was around to help you get rid of them. I'll let you walk, go ahead, keep moving... but, I will stay along the sidelines. I'll watch and I'll be here for whenever you need me."

What's that sound? It sounds like a herd of owls, one after another, they just don't stop. (*yelps, whistles, barks, and beak snaps*) And wolves! I can hear a pack of wolves! (*barks, growls, moans, snarls, whimpers, whines*) I can hear the hyper-aggressive pack of wolves! Oh goodness! I can't stop trembling, I can't move! My feet feel like a ton of bricks glued to the ground! What a way to ruin a beautiful morning!

A dreadful cloud of panic has taken over me! I know that **Fear** is near me! I'm at the edge of falling into the seducing and fascinating trap of **Temptation**! **Confusion** is around! I'm overwhelmed with a bunch of complexed and disoriented thoughts! I feel like I'm agonizing, as if I'm being tormented! **Anguish** must be around too...My body aches, I feel lightheaded, I might faint!

"No, I don't want any of you near me. Stay here, not one step further, I have to keep on moving and I need to go alone, without anyone of you accompanying me. You're all just a distraction, you're tormenting me and you keep me behind schedule!"

I feel like I need to prepare for a battle and fight these off!

I can't stand their babbling... they grunt and snort and just don't stop the chatter.... they don't come up for air, they're all talking and each one over-empowers one voice after the other directing their argument towards me.....: "We've been assigned to follow you, to be with you throughout your lifetime!" "We're not leaving, we've got nothing better to do! Well, we have been rejected by others and by some strange power, we've been expulsed from the life of millions, but we know you are gentle, you're different, and you won't reject us!" "We know, the power of our presence can sometimes scare you but we're not perfect, no one is, and all we want is to make sure that you're not alone!" "We are countless, we're many."

I need help! I need someone to help me get through this valley! This is no easy task and no one gave me a *"book of instructions"* as to how I'm supposed to handle all of this.

I feel alarmed, perplexed, astonished! They just keep popping up from everywhere! They quarrel, argue, contend and squabble all day long!

But they are a team! They sound as if they hate each other but they work together, they know exactly who is assigned to what!

What I'm understanding is that they resemble an army! They are united with strength and power. The more I entertain their voices, the greater their potential, their intensity and force!

The reality is that now I'm concerned. They've clearly identified themselves as "many" so, what else will I be faced with?

Temptation gently directs words to others that manifest and show up ahead on the road "I was wondering when you all were planning on joining us again. Did you all take a nap? Is that you, **Contention**?"

"Of course, I'm **Contention**, can't you tell? I'm ready to manifest and confront whatever and whoever, so, here I am! I'm your best defense when confrontation arises. You can have anyone of these with you but without me, your battle is lost. I'm determined to win, to have the last word, I'm full of strife and not afraid to encounter any situation."

"*Hmmmm...* not me! I'd rather not argue or even speak because my name is **Pride** and I am so special. I'm here to help you feel great! I usually team up with **Vanity** to make you feel as if you are on top of the world! We have so much to offer, more than all the others because no one is as great as we are. Well, no one is as great as I am. And, you can be as great as me, if you let me hang around."

"**Pride,** you love to be the center of attention. But we, all of us, the entire squad, we are all important. We plan on sticking with you - yup, *yesssiree.....*we are going to help you move along and cross this valley. Yup, yup, yup... I'm **Contention**, I'm very aware of all that is happening and, you need us all; all of us, just in case; and by the way, this is public territory, correct? So, we have every right to walk with you, correct? In case you didn't know, our superior, well, our father, well, he's the leader of the pack, he actually is the ruler of a kingdom. He has power and authority of the air we're breathing."

What friends? What squad? What team? What are they talking about? And, what kingdom? They babble on and on and on.

I hear it, another.... Yes, I hear a faint, shy-like voice:

"Hi, hi. You can call me **Low Self-Esteem**. I want to walk with you too. Is it alright if I do?"

"Hi **Low Self-esteem**. I might as well talk to you too. I don't know if you should walk with me. What will the others think? I do feel weak. Now that I think about it; I've never been able to accomplish anything of importance in my life. I feel like I'm not enough, I sometimes feel ashamed as to who I am."

"It's because you are insufficient. You are somewhat of a failure; correct? Think about this: if you even get to cross this valley, do you actually think you're capable of getting anything of importance done on your own? Of course not! You need me. You are not enough on your own."

"Wait, just a moment, you all need to slow down! I want to be part of this assignment. Hey you all, don't you recognize me? You're not leaving me behind. I'm **Discouragement**. You obviously cannot cross this valley without me. You are not capable of doing anything, really, but perhaps if I lead you...maybe..."

While **Guilt** got near me, I felt it was my fault that I hadn't crossed this valley yet, and with **Low Self-Esteem** near, I just feel like, like I'm not good enough. **Discouragement** isn't making my journey any better.

"I told you that you should take my advice... My name is **Temptation** for a reason... I would have helped you make a lot of progress but, you don't listen to me. Focus, think about what I've already told you. There are dangerous creatures you will face along the way, with huge sharp teeth! They're hungry and ready to hurt you! Allow me to guide you. I'll show you short cuts that no one knows about. And, we'll have a good time on the way too!"

"No thanks **Temptation**. You've been able to seduce me in the past. I've had enough of you. I'm intensely tempted but I am determined not to allow you to lure me into your traps anymore. Oh *no*! I can't handle this anymore! I know you are near, **Anxiety**, I know you are near. Get away please! In fact, all of you should leave. You are all just coming out of the woodworks! I feel an awful oppression. Your manifestations are powerful! This great weight of **Sadness** that has just poured over me is making it almost impossible for me to keep moving."

"Wait, I'm confused. Well, of course I am, my name is **Confusion**, *'hehehe'*, why are you talking to us that way? All we want is to be with you. All of us. In your past years, you accepted us, little by little. And now, now that we're united to accompany you, now that we have identified ourselves as being assigned to work in unity near you, you're rejecting us. We don't understand you."

'Haaahaa' I'm out of breath! I need to run, I can feel my heartbeat faster and faster, but I need to run. *Aggghhhhh!* '*Ouuuuch!*' This is painful! My feet hurt. '*Haaaahaaaa*' I can't keep running; I need to run and think before **Confusion** catches up to me and then I'm unable to think. '*Ouch*', '*ouch*', '*aaaaahhhhhhooooouuuch!*'

I've got to take a break. I need to rest and let my feet feel some relief. The pain is unbearable. While I rest a bit, I need to plan some kind of a defense to get away or fight them off.

I can't believe how they enjoy reminding me of my past, my mistakes, failures, and the hurt. I just don't get it! They really have an effect on my emotions, my thoughts, and my behavior!

Almost out of breath, I slow down and begin to enjoy a flatter path. Is that a small stream? Oh yeah, I'm going to rest and rinse my face, my feet and plan on how to escape from their sight.

As I walk towards the stream, I'm drawn towards my right because I think I see someone sitting, alone. Is she alone? Is she crying? I wonder if she's being tormented by the same voices? Or a bunch of different voices? Should I get close to her? Maybe I shouldn't. I think I will; I'll get near and introduce myself.

"Hi there. Are you alright?"

"Well, well I'm a little startled. And my friend is feeling panicky as well; he's over there taking a nap on the ground, a little further ahead towards my right. We're exhausted; We've been walking for a long time now and we're so lost. We're battling these strange voices in this valley and we don't know what to do to get away from them. They're tormenting us. We're in a lot of trouble and we can't fight off our situation; we're struggling to be set free of addictions but these voices just keep us involved and they don't let us go. They've hurt us, they've made us feel ashamed of ourselves and they've made us feel awful."

If she only knew that I'm facing the same battle, in a way. I think I'll act courageous and offer my help. "Well, if you allow me to walk with you and your friend, maybe the three of us can cross this valley and fight off those strange voices together."

She stares at me, and I can see her eyes, filled with tears …and she quietly responds: "You, you believe me. Thank God that you believe me!"

"Yes, of course I do! I'm facing the same situation and you are both no longer alone. We are going to figure out a way to be set free of them, all of them."

I can't believe the reaction of relief in her face. She's feeling as relieved as I am to have found her and her friend in this valley. As she stands to her feet and clenches her hands with a little perky jump she responds, "Yes, yes, please help us; but let's rest until the morning. My friend and I are so tired."

"Sure, I have this blanket, do you want to borrow it?" I only have one and even though I'll probably feel a little chilly tonight, I'm so relieved to have others to walk with and figure out a way to battle off these strange manifestations. Let me pull this blanket out of my bag. Oh, 'oops', there goes that **Book** again. I'll throw it back into my bag.

I handed my blanket over to her as she got closer to her friend. He's sound sleep. I'll step over to the left side and rest on my own.

Before I sleep, I'm going to say a prayer. *Dear God, If there is a God, if there is a God that hears me, please help me. I need you. If I've never asked you, I ask you now, I need your help. She and her friend need you as well.*

As I stare into the dark midnight-blue sky with specks of scattered lights spread all over, I can feel peace taking over me.

Chapter 6

━━◆ɛ━━━━◆●◆━━━━3◆━━

A Cry for Help Results in a Plan for Victory

It's a new morning and another opportunity for me to find success! The air feels cool and it's filled with the sweet smell of a bed of newly bloomed country flowers. As I stand up to look all around, I can see a never-ending, bright evergreen carpet that has been gently placed on the ground, decorated with dozens of clusters of bouquets mixed from beautiful and colorful flowers in perfect bloom! I can see miles and miles of the most colorful, dancing flowers, flowing gently to the movement of the morning breeze!

Why do I feel so motivated this morning? Something is happening inside of me and I can't explain it but, I'm feeling so much better! I'm not going to feel sorry for myself, I'm not going to feel any guilt, I'm not going to allow myself to be tempted, become depressed, fearful, sad, confused, anxious or discouraged! I won't become contentious, vain or be filled with pride. I can't! I need to help these others that I've found on the road. They need me. They need my help!

Today I won't be tricked by the strange voices into being involved in any of their conversations. They're not going to control me! They're incredibly destructive! Yet, I need to be realistic! I need the help of a higher being. How can I help others if I am vulnerable and fail to have the strength to fight them off? God please! Please help me! I need help, strength; I need to feel hope, I need you! If you don't help me, I won't be able to cross this valley!

We all need you! If you help me, I can help others. Well, to make it easier, give us all strength, all three of us, and anyone else walking through this valley – we need you to fight them off for us. Please?

God, I'm sorry. I'm sorry for whatever I should be sorry for. Please help me! This prayer I make in a soft whisper. I don't want anyone to hear me. But, if there's a God, this prayer will be heard. All my life, I've depended on myself; my plans, my strength, my knowledge, my wants, all about me and I have not ever asked you for your help. I have never asked you for your advice, your opinion, your direction. Time is running out and I need to cross this valley. If *these strange voices* that are *assigned* to follow me, to slow me down, to stop my success, to rob me of my peace, to destroy my happiness... continue to add others to their group, I won't make it!

Please, protect me from these evil spirits that follow me! I've wasted so much time listening to them. I admit, I've done terrible things in the past, however, I now see how I was wrong. I allowed myself to be influenced somehow, someway by more than one of them, to do wrong. And, when I became determined to cross this valley for what is "right", their voices became sharp, clear, persistent and greatly intensified. They want to stop me from getting where I need to get to.

I can't do this on my own any longer. I need help and I need it now!

The worries that I have been carrying for years, the situations that I have faced including what I face now, the oppositions that have stood before me to make life impossible for me, not allowing me to get ahead... all of this... *Can you help me?*

What is the purpose of my existence? Why was I born? If you are real, then you know that I was rejected at birth. Then, my childhood, well, it wasn't great. Did you see everything that I went through? Did you see how I was hurt? It wasn't right, none of that was right. And, did you see how I tried to do right to others and they betrayed me? I was loyal and stayed, I sat around for years, putting up with their abuse, and instead of me leaving, I was abandoned. Why did it all hurt so much? Did you see all of that? Could it be that you have plans for my existence? Could it be that you want to help me cross this valley and maybe help others to cross their own valley? There's no way that I was born to constantly struggle, or feel that I'm "not enough"... There's just no way that I was born for this! And, what about the others that I've found along the way? They don't want to be addicted to anything! They're hurting and I can see it in their eyes – the hurt, the pain, the urgency for help, they are desperate! Please help us.

God, if you exist and can hear me, please listen to me! Years ago, many years ago, someone told me that…"*we must all go through "things" in life, so that we can learn from our experiences and so that we can be "formed' to help others? Can that be so? Is that true? That person also told me that as a result of our situations or trials, we would ask you for help. I was told that you give us the right to choose from right and wrong; and, we suffer the consequences when we choose wrongly; and that you allow us to go through trials to be "molded" to who we should be, we would then surrender and start asking and depending on you, God, for help, for guidance, for approval…*"

Could it be that I've reached that moment in time when I'm supposed to ask you for help? Because, if it is so, I am serious! I am asking you for help. I am desperate! I feel weak and tired. And, I want to help the others too. If you don't help me, no one can!

As I remember the conversation with that certain person, it was explained to me that….:

God doesn't want us to suffer. However, God allows us to face difficult situations so that we may learn from our own experiences. We are only able to help others when we can truly understand what they are feeling, what they are facing. How can we if we haven't experienced anything? However, we need to surrender and ask God for help. We need to understand that God loves us and hears us; that He answers us and is but only waiting for us to ask for His help.

At one point or another in life, we all face challenges. We may face sickness, financial hardship, deception, depression…whatever we face, God can help us. He is able to turn everything that is awful, and use it for something good.

*If we are not willing to surrender our lives to God; if we are not willing to ask God for help, we are taking a high risk! For it is then when we, in our own weakness, give in to all that is offered to us. We fall into temptation; we may become corrupt, we can get filled with **Pride, Envy, Vanity, Contention, Fear,** we may be easily seduced by **Temptation** or become overwhelmed with **Anxiety, Discouragement, Depression, Sadness, Bitterness**… in short, we fall into a trap that only takes us to our own destruction.*

Wow, I feel as if my eyes are being opened; just remembering everything I was told; it's as if someone pressed a "play" button in my memory and a recording is playing back, clearly. I thought it was a bunch of nonsense. But it wasn't. I feel it inside of me; it's true, it's all true. Why did it take so many years for me to remember what I was told? I could have avoided such awful moments!

I could have asked you for help so many times! They could have too, the other two I've found in this valley. It's a good thing we found each other on the way, so we can help each other. I really want to help them. It's sad to see the hurt in her eyes; I know they've suffered, they've been hurt, they're struggling....

I'm talking to you just like I was told I could; "believing that you hear me" And you know something, God? I do believe you are listening. I can't see you but I know it, I just know that you are listening to me. ....*and I was told:* *If you surrender to God, no matter what you face, you will have peace, you will feel loved, you will feel strengthened. Wisdom and knowledge will be yours and your purpose in life will be fulfilled.... God considers us to be His children and so there are so many blessings we have the right to claim. If you are a parent, would you want to withhold anything good from your children? I would think not.*

Why would God want us to be sick? Of course He doesn't want us to be sick! He wants us to be well, however, we should learn how to ask and receive healing.

We are absolutely not supposed to "lack" anything. He wants to provide all that we need; and to give us the desires of our heart, however, in order to have access to all those good things, we need to establish a relationship with Him, as His children.

We can't go around life, ignoring God and then expect things to go so well for us. Yet, He is Love and He is Mercy, so whenever we surrender and call Him, He answers!

And just about right now, you are probably asking yourself, "How is it that I can have a relationship with God?" .... well, that happens when you open your heart and ask Him to be your God, to live in your heart and to take over your life. He speaks to us through His Word. And you are most likely asking yourself at this very moment... How do I hear His voice? You hear His voice when you read the Bible. The Bible is His Word. When you pray and ask God to help you understand what He is saying while you read the Bible, at some point, you will begin to understand what He is telling "you". You give Him authority over your life and He will lead you, He will direct your steps, He will bless you, He will heal you, he will protect you, He will guide you, He will provide for you,

He will deliver you from any temptation or danger, He will do exceedingly and abundantly more than you can imagine.

I feel so overwhelmed with peace and joy to remember all of this! The oppression I have faced has been great! I've been confused, depressed, bitter, and I can't understand how I didn't realize that a trap was prepared for me. I was being seduced, tempted, and I can't understand why I even gave any of those voices an ear! I guess that when we are not in a relationship with God, it's easy to be in a relationship with anything or anyone. I guess... it's because we're not receiving the correct instructions, and just not receiving proper guidance. Oh, how I wish I would have remembered all of this years ago!

Now that I'm thinking clearly, I can remember how without any notice, **Confusion** attacked me and took over my mind. That is a terrible manifestation and it took over me to divert me from the plans and purposes for my life.

Oh wow, I am now understanding what I was once told, that there may be times when our minds would be controlled, that we would be oppressed, without understanding what's going on; that some people live in prisons while thinking they are free; because they are controlled by these strange voices.

I'm finally being awaken. I feel like a curtain has opened and dropped before my eyes and now I have clear vision.

I can't imagine how many people are going through so many situations and think there's no way out; or truly believe that life isn't worth living or maybe are even convinced that they deserve to be in the situation that they're in! If I could only tell the world! If I could only help rescue one person at a time... to tell them, to help them... there has to be a way that I can help!

God, are you still listening to me? If you are listening, I just want to tell you how thankful and relieved I am. Thank you for opening my eyes and reminding me that I can ask you for help.

It's amazing; just how in an instant, my life has been refreshed with a *wake-up* call. It's as if God has poured out an ocean of love and mercy over me. (*gently wiping the tears rolling down both sides of my eyes*) Ok now, I don't want the others to see me tearing. Just yesterday I felt as if I didn't have a way out, that I had no hope but today, everything has changed! (*while smiling and with a light happy giggle*) I can cry all I want now, but of relief!

Just yesterday, I felt like my life was not worth living; I felt as if I might as well put an end to it because I hadn't done anything right in my life anyway, so why bother waiting for anything else to occur?

Just yesterday, I felt miserable! I felt as if I had no answers to what I was going through; I felt as if nothing could give me peace or that no one could bring happiness near me; I felt as if I had made so many wrong decisions in life that caused me to lose out on so much and so I must be "*not enough*" or not be a good person. But, this morning, I want to cry because I feel - I feel it inside of me! I can be happy! I have so much to live for! There's a reason for all I've gone through! There's a purpose for my being - I have life for a great purpose! I need to help others!

And, as if...I can hear the voice of the beautiful continued conversation telling me years ago... "*There's help for all the oppressed, all the depressed, there's help for the heartbroken, for the sad, for the one who is hurting; there's help for the one carrying a great weight of guilt, anguish or anger; there's help!*

There's a true evil enemy that enjoys tormenting us; that would love for us to go through life without ever discovering the secret to true joy, the secret to being delivered from all evil; the secret to being set free of all that robs us of joy, peace, happiness, true success... there's a simple secret that isn't shared much...In the middle of a storm, you can have peace! Although we will face trials, we can feel joy! Problems show up in everyone's life, but we can face all things with strength, joy, peace...... so, I want to share with you:

If you are ever walking through dry land, if you ever feel alone, if you ever go through a season of anxiety, if you ever feel like a failure, if you are ever wronged, if you are ever rejected or mistreated or abused, if you are ever in need, if you are ever sick or addicted to anything in any way.... remember, there's help for you! God wants to help you and he can take care of anything and everything, you just have to ask Him for help.

Don't try to carry the load on your own. Don't be filled with pride that you won't ask God for help. Just talk to Him, wherever you are at, just talk to Him!

You don't have to be in a special place or inside a specific building or with anyone present - just find a place, a quiet place and talk to God. God is your Heavenly Father; He is the author of life! He created you; and He is waiting for you! He's so loving and kind and merciful and wants to help you but He's not rude.

He's not about to interfere if you don't want His help. He's courteous, he'll let you choose; He'll let you decide whether or not you want His help. Just talk to Him!

God is amazing! He will fill any void. There's no need to walk around feeling lonely; ashamed; guilty; or unwanted. He is waiting for you to ask for help.

Oh yeah - I can remember that during the beginning of my journey, all of these terrible voices reminded me of so many awful things! I was out of breath most of the time. I would wake up in the middle of the night with uncomfortable sweats! Fatigued! I was anxious, worried, and discouraged.

I was reminded of terrible things that I went through, of all the pain I've experienced; emotionally, for so many years. It was as if the most minimal thing, smell, sound, color or place would bring those bad memories back to me over and over again.

And how many years did I walk around feeling that I was not good enough? I tried to succeed in so many ways, yet I failed. I had such low self-esteem.

The amount of wrong decisions I made are countless! These all brought about consequences, negative consequences. I've cried, I've been angry, I've been depressed...

What about all the times that I was sincere and true but was betrayed? It happened so many times that I became cold - I felt as if I should never trust anyone ever again. Feeling rejected isn't pleasant, being lied to is awful, and being betrayed hurts but I haven't been perfect either. I too have made mistakes and I've carried so much guilt and no matter what I've done - there's that voice that comes back to haunt me.

I feel as if I'm always battling something. I've tried everything and anything that has been offered to me to try to be happy. How many "happy hours" have I gone to thinking I was going to feel happy, only to be left feeling so empty inside.

There's no bar, club, or entertainment whatsoever that brings true happiness - it's all a temporary *"fix"* - it's not a permanent or true solution.

When one addiction wasn't enough, I tried another - trying to fill that void.

It seemed that everyone around me was succeeding and getting everything that I've ever wanted - and me....*well*, just sitting on the sideline waiting for things to happen.

Some of the people that have hurt me are the closest to me; family, friends, loved ones. I've tried to forgive and forget but the emotional damage just reappears!

I've watched families fall apart; businesses fail; best friends that turn against one another. I've gone to bed crying, desperately wondering "what's next"?

What about when I was sick and no one knew exactly how I felt. I had to transfer money from one credit card to another, sell personal belongings and do whatever I needed to do to get by - well, that was not easy but that was the easiest stuff to handle. The thought of *"what if"* I don't get better; *"what if I don't make it"*; *"I don't have anything to leave to my family if I die"*...and I had no one to talk to. I felt so much anguish. I went from having words spinning in my mind to feeling disappointed in myself and crying myself to sleep.

Being abandoned by someone you love marks you for life! Or at least that is what I thought, until now! There's no reason to walk around forever with so much hurt!

All of these memories sounded over and over when these strange voices persisted, insisting in reminding me of my past!

I have not been able to forgive myself for so many things. But today, I am reminded that if God forgives me, why should I continue carrying so much guilt? It's time to forgive myself. I need to feel free and I can!

Those evil voices were truly assigned to torment me! They are part of the enemy's camp; they are assigned to hurt us, to destroy us, to take away our peace, our joy, our success, our health, our loved ones, and our life itself. But today I'm reminded that God does not bring back the memory of your past to hurt you! God wants to set us free of what hurts to restore us, to bless us so that we may prosper in all of our ways. I feel so great this morning! I have hope!

Once we are convinced by those strange voices, we are trapped. We feel imprisoned, we feel blocked, we feel that there's no way out, we feel that we have no other choice but to accept all the negative... but it is all a lie!

I was weak for so long! - I was so close to being convinced by **Temptation**! **Temptation** is very convincing and so many of us are deceived and get profoundly involved and entangled in such messes!

Nothing can compare with what God has to offer us. There's no evil, there's no money, no position, no business, no partnership, no riches, no material wealth, no person, nothing on this earth that can compare with all that God has to offer, if we just ask Him for help!

I'm going to get up, pick up this backpack and wake up the others. I'm going to help them! I have a plan and we're going to succeed!

Chapter 7

A Decision to Take Action

The happy babbling and rushing whisper of the stream served as my alarm clock to this new day. It's time to stand to my feet and walk over to wake-up the other two. "Hey, good morning. Did you sleep well? I think we should get started." She and her friend both hear me and open their eyes with a look of relief, a faint smile; they're probably as glad to see me as I am to see that they're still here near me. While they wash their faces with the cool clean stream waters…. I'm standing here, looking around to see in which direction we should begin to walk; wondering which is the best path; oh, is there a compass in my backpack? Pulling things out of my bag and pushing them back in…a compass? Yes? No?…. And what is this **Book** about? I quickly swing it open to the middle and a note drops out of it that reads:

*May you find all of the answers you need in this **Book**, just as I did. Everything that I ever shared with you: advice, counsel, knowledge, and information, I learned from this **Book**. Of course, there were many things I didn't understand but with faith in God, I asked for His help and I received revelation of what is written.*

*You need this **Book**. In fact, everyone does. Please read it, study it, learn from it, treasure it, and you will find that there is nothing you cannot face because this **Book** gives you power, authority and instructions for each life-situation. Inside this **Book** is your answer, your key to true love, joy, freedom, healing, success, and whatever it is that you need; it is all found in this **Book**.*

I can't believe it! Everything my friend talked to me about, he learned from this **Book**. I have one at home that I have not read for so many years. In fact, I have no idea where it is.

It's all making sense to me now. Had I given the value it is worthy of, had I applied what this **Book** instructs... *I can't even think, I'm so overwhelmed...*

Sure, of course I have read small parts of this **Book** but I thought it was just a book, something filled with personal opinions.... I never thought it was so important, valuable or had any power. It's because I was so busy. I was busy living my way, with my choices, my thoughts, my ideas...

I'm remembering my friend; sharing his knowledge with me, and advising me:

*When we apply what is learned through this **Book**, we receive true help, the best solutions, and blessings.*

*Oftentimes, we make our experience while we gather inside a church building, something more social. We attend, we sing, we hear a sermon, but how much do we learn? How much do we study the Word of God while we are home? How many of us ask God for a revelation that can only come from Him while we read this **Book**?*

It's time, it's my time; and I've reached a point in my journey, in my life, where I now realize that I am ready to accept that I need to know what is written in this **Book**. I need to understand it and I need to apply it to my life. What is written in this **Book** is compared to a two-edge sword! Had I used that sword during my journey, I would have had a better trip! Each time a strange voice came near me, I needed that sword, I could have used it for protection. Once you use that sword, all strange voices debilitate, and they must vanish...

Hebrews 4:12-13
[12] For the word of God is quick, and powerful, and sharper than any two-edged sword, piercing even to the dividing asunder of soul and spirit, and of the joints and marrow, and is a discerner of the thoughts and intents of the heart.
[13] Neither is there any creature that is not manifest in his sight: but all things are naked and opened unto the eyes of him with whom we have to do.

Our words don't scare anyone; our words don't scare strange voices, or our enemies. However, when we declare what is written in the Word of God, our enemies tremble.

The Word of God has authority and power.

> Isaiah 55:11
> [11] So shall my word be that goeth forth out of my mouth: it shall not return unto me void, but it shall accomplish that which I please, and it shall prosper in the thing whereto I sent it. (The sword)

Don't doubt that God's word has effect; it is powerful!

Throughout my journey, this is all I needed, but it's never too late! **I now have a great plan and I will put it into action!**

I'm no longer going to fear the strange voices that were tormenting me; the obstacles that I faced. All of those strange voices were assigned - they were sent by the enemy of all souls, to stop me - to destroy me; and they succeeded for a while! For some time, I was weakened, they identified themselves and I entertained them, I thought I was smart enough and had enough strength to control my walk, to control my life, but I was weak and I failed to use the "sword" that I once had heard about. I never even gave the Word of God any importance. I never gave it the value it deserved!

Life is a school of experiences and we can all use some help. The Word of God is the weapon that we have been left with to protect us throughout our lives. The knowledge of understanding the meaning of the Word of God and the wisdom to apply it upon our lives is our key to success and victory.

We have no idea as to when we're going to go through a "valley " - through trials, hardship, pain, or sorrow. For this reason, we need to have answers ready, to know what is written by God, to use it whenever we need it.

Sometimes we feel self-sufficient and let go of our weapon (The Word of God). It is then when we lose battles.

When we put our weapon to aside, when we stop reading the Word of God, when we stop studying and searching for answers in His Word, and when we stop believing what He says, we fall into traps and danger.

Our journey is a walk through a battlefield. We all don't face the same enemies; we all don't face the same attacks, but at some point in life, we do face adversity. God wants us to be armed and use His Word as our weapon.

When we spend time with God by reading and studying His Word; and by praying and asking him for the interpretation; we learn - we learn how to face each battle.

> 1 Samuel 2:30
> [30] Wherefore the LORD God of Israel saith, I said indeed that thy house, and the house of thy father, should walk before me for ever: but now the LORD saith, Be it far from me; for them that honour me I will honour, and they that despise me shall be lightly esteemed.

Regardless of what others may think or say, God has not abandoned me. God was waiting for me to make a decision. I had to make haste, I had to stop wavering, my condition was an "emergency" but God gave me the opportunity to make a decision.

We have the ability to live experiencing true peace, true contentment, true love, and true success. There's a simple way to do this. It's a decision. In a second, we make a decision for either life or death. If we make a decision for life, we make the decision to accept Jesus as our savior; a simple prayer rejecting sin and accepting Christ - that is the beginning. Then, we begin to keep a daily means of communication with God which will establish a relationship between us. You can't have a relationship with anyone without communication. We can either pray, study His Word, which is the Bible, congregate, and or worship Him through songs. When we strengthen our relationship with God, we are able to recognize the dangerous traps of the enemy. This way of living leads us to the path of divine purpose of God for us.

I was near losing out on all the good, all of the blessings, and all the promises that God has for me. What can be more valuable than salvation - the guarantee of eternal life? Forgiveness of my sins? The guarantee of peace that surpasses all human understanding?

God's mercy saved me. I need to be armed always with the power of His Word. I now understand that what I need to reach victory, to be triumphant, is to walk with the knowledge on how to use my weapon/ The Word of God.

> 2 Corinthians 10:4-5
> [4] (For the weapons of our warfare are not carnal, but mighty through God to the pulling down of strong holds;)
> [5] Casting down imaginations, and every high thing that exalteth itself against the knowledge of God, and bringing into captivity every thought to the obedience of Christ;

We can't fight with our words, or with physical actions. We can't successfully operate in a battlefield if we are not armed with the Word of God. Our enemies will defeat us and we'll lose out on all that God has for us.

A soldier needs preparation, and needs training, and this is the exact position we are in. We must be trained, and we must prepare ourselves for battle. We don't know when we'll face a struggle, but we will.

So many have gone out into the battlefield without the armor of God, without the weapon that God has given us, and they have been defeated by the enemy. Others are still battling, however, with the wrong weapons; they are fighting on their own, with their own strengths, with their own weapons.

Many believe that our military has an overly rigid training regimen; however, if it were not this way, they would not be prepared to win; they would not have a chance of survival!

If our military did not receive or follow the proper training, we would be mocked and defeated by our enemies. Can you imagine?

If our military members can follow instructions, just on the fact that they are taught that if they do what they are trained to, they will defeat the enemy, then, why can't we follow their example? God leaves a book of instructions for us and that is the Bible. It is a book of instructions for every single situation we face in life, in our journey. If we follow His instructions, if we understand, believe and do what the Bible instructs us to, we can face any battle and have victory.

Matthew 11:28-30

²⁸ Come unto me, all ye that labour and are heavy laden, and I will give you rest.

²⁹ Take my yoke upon you, and learn of me; for I am meek and lowly in heart: and ye shall find rest unto your souls.

³⁰ For my yoke is easy, and my burden is light.

For all that I've been through, I definitely need rest! I feel like I've been through a series of storms. It's awful to walk without a sense of security, feel blind-folded, and be pursued by strange voices following close behind to destroy me. It's been a nightmare but I feel like I should share my story so that others don't walk their journey without help. Others need to know that if they walk alone, without the proper weapons, they will be fighting a losing battle - sooner or later, it's death for sure.

It's never too late to have your mind "renewed":

Ephesians 4:23-24

²³ And be renewed in the spirit of your mind;

²⁴ And that ye put on the new man, which after God is created in righteousness and true holiness.

Thank God that my mind has been renewed. I feel such a great change in my life. Although I am physically weak, I have been wounded and feel pain, I am sure that God is going to heal me.

Psalm 103:1-6

103 Bless the LORD, O my soul: and all that is within me, bless his holy name.

² Bless the LORD, O my soul, and forget not all his benefits:

³ Who forgiveth all thine iniquities; who healeth all thy diseases;

⁴ Who redeemeth thy life from destruction; who crowneth thee with lovingkindness and tender mercies;

⁵ Who satisfieth thy mouth with good things; so that thy youth is renewed like the eagle's.

⁶ The LORD executeth righteousness and judgment for all that are oppressed.

We should not ever forget that God offers benefits to us. When we feel we're sinking, we can depend on God to rescue us, because he is merciful.

Ephesians 6:10-17

¹⁰ Finally, my brethren, be strong in the Lord, and in the power of his might.

¹¹ Put on the whole armour of God, that ye may be able to stand against the wiles of the devil.

¹² For we wrestle not against flesh and blood, but against principalities, against powers, against the rulers of the darkness of this world, against spiritual wickedness in high places.

¹³ Wherefore take unto you the whole armour of God, that ye may be able to withstand in the evil day, and having done all, to stand.

¹⁴ Stand therefore, having your loins girt about with truth, and having on the breastplate of righteousness;

¹⁵ And your feet shod with the preparation of the gospel of peace;

¹⁶ Above all, taking the shield of faith, wherewith ye shall be able to quench all the fiery darts of the wicked.

¹⁷ And take the helmet of salvation, and the sword of the Spirit, which is the word of God:

Who goes to war without being properly dressed?... Without the proper uniform? ...Without the necessary weapons? It just does not make any sense to face an army without knowledge, instructions, or proper training.

During times of war, we can be identified by our uniform and by our techniques. We should be dressed with the armor of God and use as a weapon, His Word - which is a two-edge sword.

We are easily identified by our enemies. Who are we walking with? How is our walk, our talk...?

We often times walk with people that detain us. They are assigned to our journey to distract us, to drain us, to be an obstacle in our divine purpose. Their purpose in our path is to cause detours, problems, setbacks, and anything that will stop God's divine purpose for us.

The enemy and his demonic army work against us. He sets many traps to fulfill his purpose: to destroy us.

We can't give ear to the strange voices. We cannot give Satan the slightest opportunity because he is no respecter and he will barge in if we give him the most minute opportunity. We can't entertain him or his agents, at all!

There may be times, during your journey, when someone gets close to you and befriends you. This person may show you kindness, may hug you, may show that your best interest is in mind, however, it may be the enemy setting you up for a trap. Now, this is not always the case. I am just giving you an example as to what happens often.

It doesn't matter where you meet someone. Ask God for direction and guidance at all times. God reveals all things to us, when we ask Him to.

It is so common that we want to share what we're going through, because we need someone to trust, we need someone to hear what trials we're facing. So, we connect with someone that we think is trustworthy. And, because we chose that person, without going to God first for direction, we are often led in the wrong direction with the wrong advice... because it was a trap set up for us by the enemy of all souls.

The Word of God advises us:

Jeremiah 17:5
⁵ Thus saith the LORD; Cursed be the man that trusteth in man, and maketh flesh his arm, and whose heart departeth from the LORD.

At times, we may fall into the trap of the deceiver and by trusting the wrong people, we open those doors. It's when we are so emotionally involved with the wrong people that we suddenly realize we're in some type of awful trouble. We may be hurt, saddened, confused, or angry and we are then visited by **Discouragement** and **Bitterness** and we may even receive the visitation of **Temptation** that tells us we should seek vengeance. We are advised by the wrong strange voices. And then, we might even receive hugs by **Fear**. **Low-self-esteem** makes an entrance to camp out for a while with us. Soon thereafter, we begin to feel that we aren't worth much. It is an army sent to attack us by the Devil himself!

Jeremiah 17:6
6 For he shall be like the heath in the desert, and shall not see when good cometh; but shall inhabit the parched places in the wilderness, in a salt land and not inhabited.

It is tremendous - terrible to be that shrub in the desert, that does not attract anything good; having no growth, no admiration, in arid land. Who would care for something like this? Not many.

God wants to be your help, rescue you, be your oasis, provide all of your needs, lift you up and exhibit you like a beautiful tree that grows and has much fruit.

Psalm 121:2-4
2 My help cometh from the LORD, which made heaven and earth.
3 He will not suffer thy foot to be moved: he that keepeth thee will not slumber.
4 Behold, he that keepeth Israel shall neither slumber nor sleep.

Psalm 46:1-2
God is our refuge and strength, a very present help in trouble.
2 Therefore will not we fear, though the earth be removed, and though the mountains be carried into the midst of the sea;

We can't open the door to **Confusion** because we will surely be taken over by an uneasy mindset and feel lost.

It is necessary that we communicate, daily, with God, so that we grow in wisdom, knowledge, understanding, and discernment.

Our battlefield is our mind. Therefore, we must renew our mind on a daily basis with our communication with God. When we lose that communication with God, the enemy sees that the coast is clear and enters to attack us. The enemy enters with a variety of weapons: *distractions, fear, detours, confusion, anxiety, depression, loneliness,* just to name a few. It is then that we are so weakened that we can't see clearly. We continue to walk while debilitated and continue to walk in the path of the enemy. The longer we walk without the help of God, the more the enemies that are assigned against you, more evil spirits, all united and strengthened to work towards the Devil's main purpose: to destroy you.

God is waiting on us to talk to him. He wants to rescue us from whatever we're struggling with.

God's Word is filled with blessings, and He is waiting for someone to claim those blessings. It's similar to someone who is ill and is given a prescription and then fails to claim the medication at the pharmacy and would rather continue with the illness. We have a choice. Do we continue to walk without the blessings or do we grab them all since they are ours anyway?

God wants us to receive fullness of joy, peace that surpasses all human understanding, healing and so much more.

Well, I've made a decision, I'm not going to be destroyed by strange voices. I'm going to be strengthened by what is written in God's word and I'm going to win this battle. I'm also going to help others!

Chapter 8

A Struggle with My Enemies

I think I'll share some things with the other two I've found along this journey. "Hey, before we begin our walk today, I'd like to share some things with you both. I'm not sure how you're going to take all that I have to share, but it is good news, I want you both to prepare for battle, and I want you both to be able to defeat your enemies."

They both sit back down on the ground in almost a manner of *'sure, what do we have to lose? We've gone through so much, we're helpless, we need answers, please, help us'*…. And they both glance at each other and then at the same time, look over at me, giving me the *'go ahead, talk'* look… and so I begin to share with them:

If we are ready to face the opposition, and fight for our deliverance, then it is necessary to know how to detect our enemies. When we receive that revelation, when we are able to distinguish who is for us and who is against us, we can prepare for our struggle and prepare for victory.

When we fail to detect our enemy, when we are unable to understand that they are strange voices used by the Devil, when we cannot understand who an agent of Satan is or identify when a trap has been set for us, then we lose out! We may accept our enemies as our allies, we become their slaves, we may begin to lose our memory and we soon forget that God is the only one who can set us free from bondage and trials.

God offers us freedom. He delivers us from our past sins, curses, sickness, addictions, and all oppression sent by the enemy.

The enemy has the contrary in mind for us; he wants to enslave us; he wants to keep us in bondage.

Keep in mind that when someone decides to walk away from a fleshly way of life, a carnal lifestyle, and decides to accept Jesus as savior, the windows, doors and gates of *hades* are opened with an army of demons assigned to stop God's work in that person's life. Therefore, it is so important to know that when we accept Jesus Christ as our Lord and savior, and when we totally surrender to God, He seals us with His Holy Spirit. We then become heirs of our Heavenly Father, and we are given a special covering, a divine protection. Not only are we armed with the Word of God, not only are we sealed by the Spirit of God, but he charges angels over us, an army of warrior angels and guardian angels to protect us. We are also covered by the blood of Jesus. It is not a physical covering, it is a divine covering; a covering that cleanses us of all sin, of all sickness and disease.

The Word of God renews our mind. The renewing of our mind gives us insight, it gives us revelation and we become aware to so much we were blinded to in our past. You see, we suddenly become fully equipped for our journey, a journey called life, and when we step out into that journey, a journey that oftentimes is filled with darkness, then we are no longer helpless, we are no longer weak, because when we are weak, we are made strong in Christ; and our help comes from the Lord; and victory is surely ours!

When we fail to study the Word of God, we fail to understand how we may be strengthened, we fail to understand how to operate properly in life for success. I want to make it clear, that the Word of God is a *Guide to Life Manual*.

2 Corinthians 10:4-5
[4] (For the weapons of our warfare are not carnal, but mighty through God to the pulling down of strong holds;)
[5] Casting down imaginations, and every high thing that exalteth itself against the knowledge of God, and bringing into captivity every thought to the obedience of Christ;

Let us arm ourselves with the Word of God, the sword of the spirit.

Ephesians 6:17

17 And take the helmet of salvation, and the sword of the
Spirit, which is the word of God.

The Word of God is God's authority. Everything God says needs to
be used for the destruction of all evil forces.

Our enemy is Satan. He and his kingdom, his agents, demonic army
and evil forces have their plans to declare war against us. But he also
knows that we no longer belong to him. Once we accept Jesus as our
savior, we become property of God; we become part of the Kingdom of
God and that makes Jesus our King.

Whether Satan likes it or not, he has to bow down to the name of
Jesus. Jesus spoke to Satan when he fasted:

Matthew 4:4-10

4 But he answered and said, It is written, Man shall not
live by bread alone, but by every word that proceedeth
out of the mouth of God.

5 Then the devil taketh him up into the holy city, and
setteth him on a pinnacle of the temple,

6 And saith unto him, If thou be the Son of God, cast
thyself down: for it is written, He shall give his angels
charge concerning thee: and in their hands they shall
bear thee up, lest at any time thou dash thy foot against
a stone.

7 Jesus said unto him, It is written again, Thou shalt not
tempt the Lord thy God.

8 Again, the devil taketh him up into an exceeding high
mountain, and sheweth him all the kingdoms of the
world, and the glory of them;

9 And saith unto him, All these things will I give thee, if
thou wilt fall down and worship me.

10 Then saith Jesus unto him, Get thee hence, Satan: for
it is written, Thou shalt worship the Lord thy God, and
him only shalt thou serve.

Yes, of course we have to eat to survive, however, there's another kind of nourishment, a spiritual nourishment.

We can't have a life of victory and success without the knowledge of God's word. Satan is very much aware of the word of God and he knows that he does not have to bow down to our words but he must, without a choice, surrender to the word of God.

Not for a moment should we be unarmed. The word of God is a sword, it is our weapon.

We also ought to be doers of the Word of God:

James 1:22-25
[22] But be ye doers of the word, and not hearers only, deceiving your own selves.
[23] For if any be a hearer of the word, and not a doer, he is like unto a man beholding his natural face in a glass:
[24] For he beholdeth himself, and goeth his way, and straightway forgetteth what manner of man he was.
[25] But whoso looketh into the perfect law of liberty, and continueth therein, he being not a forgetful hearer, but a doer of the work, this man shall be blessed in his deed.

When we speak the word of God, it becomes active, because it is alive. Therefore, we can see demons get uncomfortable but all that rises up against the will of God, falls.

What God has established, nothing nor no one can revoke, cancel or destroy. With His Word, we have the authority to captivate all of the powers of darkness, whether it be sickness, depression, confusion, and anything that is contrary to what the Word of God says about us.

We cannot give an ear to what the enemy says against us, for we are children of the great living God. We've been bought with a great price... yes, the precious blood of Jesus paid for us!

Again, reading, studying and applying the Word of God, keeps us armed. It is a weapon, a sword, that keeps us on guard - warned, and always makes a way for our victory throughout our journey.

It is a big deal, a big problem to face difficulty and be found unarmed. That is why so often offers made by the enemy: to accept depression, bitterness, rejection, anxiety... leaves us with no other choice, because the weapon is not available to us to fight them off. God wants you to be armed always.

At times we become tired, weak, and even exhausted. We're so debilitated that there's no way we can fight off the enemy. We try to struggle on our own, but those attacks assigned by the kingdom of Satan are too strong. We try, we cry, we get desperate, but we are unarmed and so we are defeated.

However, I have great news! We all have the right to accept victory. We are all given the choice to be armed with God's power, God's authority, God's weapon, so that we can be valiant, courageous and face our battles and struggle with our enemies, without doubting that we will not be defeated!

Chapter 9

--ε·------·◦◄●►·◦·----·3◄----

A Plan for Our Guaranteed Success is Revealed

We should understand that life is not a dress-rehearsal, that this is it! We get one chance and we should live according to what is written in God's word:

> Psalm 23
> 23 The LORD is my shepherd; I shall not want.
> ² He maketh me to lie down in green pastures: he leadeth me beside the still waters.
> ³ He restoreth my soul: he leadeth me in the paths of righteousness for his name's sake.
> ⁴ Yea, though I walk through the valley of the shadow of death, I will fear no evil: for thou art with me; thy rod and thy staff they comfort me.
> ⁵ Thou preparest a table before me in the presence of mine enemies: thou anointest my head with oil; my cup runneth over.
> ⁶ Surely goodness and mercy shall follow me all the days of my life: and I will dwell in the house of the LORD forever.

A portion of God's word, Psalm 23, is shared all in different circumstances; for meditating when needing peace, to console in time of sorrow, to motivate - a chapter to admire, value and understand the message that is filled for hope of life and victory.

We are all attacked in one way or another, we cannot judge anyone, ever, for whatever they go through. One day, we may also face oppositions.

When we meditate in the word of Psalm 23, we understand its contents; that it is a lesson of how we can use it to defeat the enemy.

The shepherd cares for his sheep; so, whenever there's a prowler, or any beast that is ready to attack and devour the sheep, he is there to protect his sheep and destroy the enemy. He fights for his sheep!

The Psalmist, David, said: The Lord is my shepherd. He said it with confidence and security. This is what our heart knows for sure; that we know that God will fulfill whatever His Word says.

God is able to provide all things to us. That is why when we need something, we have the faith that whatever we ask for, we receive. God doesn't want us to lack anything:

Philippians 4:19
[19] But my God shall supply all your need according to his riches in glory by Christ Jesus

When we know what the Word of God says, when we treasure it in our heart, we can walk and live counting on whatever God says.

God does not leave us in a state of *"not enough"*. He is well aware of all of our needs.

Matthew 11:28
[28] Come unto me, all ye that labour and are heavy laden, and I will give you rest.

True rest is when we can have peace in the middle of adversity, in the midst of a great problem, because we will not be shaken, we will not doubt, we will not get desperate, we will not lose trust and hope in what the word of God tells us.

The Lord is our peace, our true rest, our refuge and help.

Going back into the Old Testament, we see Moses talking to God; and God tells Moses that he will take His people out of Egypt. What a great responsibility. Moses knew that without God, he could not do this. He knew he needed God's direction and God's help.

Moses needed an answer from God:

Exodus 33:12-14

¹² And Moses said unto the Lord, See, thou sayest unto me, Bring up this people: and thou hast not let me know whom thou wilt send with me. Yet thou hast said, I know thee by name, and thou hast also found grace in my sight. ¹³ Now therefore, I pray thee, if I have found grace in thy sight, shew me now thy way, that I may know thee, that I may find grace in thy sight: and consider that this nation is thy people. ¹⁴ And he said, My presence shall go with thee, and I will give thee rest.

The call and purpose Moses had was not an easy one. It carried great weight, great responsibility, and he had to be devoted. For this same reason, many ministers and leaders called by God, leave their careers and businesses to answer to God's call.

When the leader goes through a valley, when the leader loses a loved one, when the leader is rejected or mistreated, when the leader is suffering.... he continues to fulfill his call. A minister of God also faces giants and perhaps the biggest giants... yet, he does not give up, he just continues for his responsibility is great.

Don't be intimidated by your enemies or by the darts thrown at you by them. Don't just sit and let the enemy walk all over you. Get up and put up a fight because you can't win a battle if you don't even try!

Don't let the enemy rob you of your victory or your position as a child in the Kingdom of God.

If you are a minister or a leader, I say the same to you.... do not, by any means, do not lose your position when you face opposition. We are formed in the desert; we are formed in the storm; we are formed through trials and attacks; and that is how we become true champions.

When we trust God, we must do our part in the battle. We pray and we confess the Word of God, while we ask Him for help.

Have you ever observed an animal sitting near his newborn? You have to be careful not to touch that newborn because his parent will give you a run for your life!

In the same manner, God fights for his children; God fights for us! The Psalmist David said:

Psalm 34:4-7

[4] I sought the LORD, and he heard me, and delivered me from all my fears.

[5] They looked unto him, and were lightened: and their faces were not ashamed.

[6] This poor man cried, and the LORD heard him, and saved him out of all his troubles.

[7] The angel of the LORD encampeth round about them that fear him, and delivereth them.

When we make a decision to walk in the path of the Lord, we are surprised by unexpected trials, attacks, and strange voices that try to intimidate us. We will be visited by *uninvited* strangers. These are spirits that fight against our lives. However, we don't have to welcome their visitation. We must be able to quickly identify them and close the doors to them, immediately.

The difference between the person that walks with God and the person that does not have a relationship with God is that one knows how to face the storm and be triumphant and the other does not. One person may be overcome by fear and the other knows how to tell fear to leave.

Psalm 91:1-2

91 He that dwelleth in the secret place of the most High shall abide under the shadow of the Almighty.

[2] I will say of the LORD, He is my refuge and my fortress: my God; in him will I trust.

We often forget that as children of God, property of God, we have a special covering. What kind of covering is that? To abide under the shadow of the Almighty is a covering that cannot be compared to any other. There is no other protection that is superior to the shadow of the Almighty!

Psalm 34:8
⁸ O taste and see that the LORD is good: blessed is the man that trusteth in him

It is good to trust in the Lord. We can trust Him with all things.

It is normal for us to trust our friends and family, however, they may all fail us but God never fails us.

It is normal that at one point or another in life, we share our difficulties with a friend or someone we are close to. We may be battling an addiction, a disease, or other struggle. Sometimes we are helped and sometimes we continue in the same condition, no matter how much others try to help us. Yet, there is someone who will guide us correctly; that will respond with love; that will never reject us or judge us; one that we can call on at any time as many times as we need; that we can confide in:

Psalm 23:3
³ He restoreth my soul: he leadeth me in the paths of righteousness for his name's sake.

It is necessary that we face the storms; go through difficult situations; and even face the attacks of the enemy because it is then that we get to know how great God's love is for us. He is our comforter, He is our strength, He is always with us. And yes, we ask ourselves as to why we go through such difficult situations, such painful moments. Sometimes we are responsible for our wrong decision and sometimes, He allows us to experience such things. However, it is necessary that we experience the trials so that we get to know who God is, how much he loves us, and how powerful He is. We are vessels that are going through a process of formation. Each time we conquer a battle, we are formed a little better; we become better persons. God will always use whatever you go through for a testimony, to help others that are going through or will go through the same situation you went through.

Romans 8:28

[28] And we know that all things work together for good to them that love God, to them who are the called according to his purpose.

2 Corinthians 1:3-4

[3] Blessed be God, even the Father of our Lord Jesus Christ, the Father of mercies, and the God of all comfort;

[4] Who comforteth us in all our tribulation, that we may be able to comfort them which are in any trouble, by the comfort wherewith we ourselves are comforted of God.

This is a word of hope! It doesn't matter where you are at, in what condition you are in, there is hope!

Psalm 46:1-2

God is our refuge and strength, a very present help in trouble.

[2] Therefore will not we fear, though the earth be removed, and though the mountains be carried into the midst of the sea;

We can't forget who is our help. Whenever we face a battle, we go into our treasure chest, which is our heart, where we have hidden the word of God... and then we are reminded where our help comes from!

Psalm 23:4

[4] Yea, though I walk through the valley of the shadow of death, I will fear no evil: for thou art with me; thy rod and thy staff they comfort me.

The Word of God instructs us to wear the armor of God, to use the shield of faith, to use the Word of God by speaking what it says and not what we see or what others say. We have the weapon, the strategies to be victorious always.

Our journey, *life*, will include opposition. But when fear, confusion, insecurity or any opposition arrives, we have a defense.

Our journey, *life*, will also include strange voices that are direct darts of the enemy, assigned to hurt us, to distract us, and to ruin us. But now, we know that we have instructions, through the Bible, through the Word of God on how to fight against each and every attack.

So often we think we don't have a purpose. That is a lie – *the Devil is a liar!* **You have a purpose in life! God loves each one of us and He has created you with purpose!** The reason we are convinced that we don't is because we give ear to the strange voices that Satan and his demons send to block us, to stop God's purpose with us.

Psalm 27:1-3

The LORD is my light and my salvation; whom shall I fear? the LORD is the strength of my life; of whom shall I be afraid?

² When the wicked, even mine enemies and my foes, came upon me to eat up my flesh, they stumbled and fell.

³ Though an host should encamp against me, my heart shall not fear: though war should rise against me, in this will I be confident.

Luke 10:19

¹⁹ Behold, I give unto you power to tread on serpents and scorpions, and over all the power of the enemy: and nothing shall by any means hurt you.

God's word is great, it is amazing and he has opened my eyes and made me free! God has given me authority and power through His Word to fight all opposition. *Time to fight*:

Confusion: You have no power over me and my mind; In the name of Jesus, I tell you to leave and that I am free of you.

Depression: You are defeated because Jesus has set me free. You are not welcome to join me ever again. I close all doors that ever allowed you to visit me. I'm evicting you from my life, permanently!

Sadness: The joy of the Lord is my Strength! Sadness, I reject you now in the name of Jesus.

Fear: You are an evil spirit sent to torment me and stop God's purpose in my life but I speak to you with the authority given to me by God in His Word and I tell you to flee. I am free to live a life with purpose.

Anguish: In the name of Jesus: I tell you to get away from me; you cannot walk with me. You are not welcomed in my life, in my journey.

Bitterness: Your walk with me is done. You are not part of my life and I reject you right now. Flee right now, in the name of Jesus!

Guilt: Your assignment to burden me is finished because God has forgiven me. In the name of Jesus: Go back to where you came from and you do not have my permission to return by my side!

Temptation: In the name of Jesus, I tell you, with all of your purposes, and all of your companions, get away and do not return! Because of God's power over my life, I am free of you and all of your assigned companions.

Pride and Vanity: I am free of you and your influences. I order you to flee in the name of Jesus!

Discouragement: You were defeated when Jesus died for me on the cross. I order you to leave me, you have no power over me in the name of Jesus.

Contention: I am free of all evil spirits. You have no authority or power over me! In Jesus' name.

Curse: I say to you in the name of Jesus: I am free of all curses; my children are free of all curses; my grandchildren are free of all curses; I cancel all curses spoken against me and my family. I am free of afflictions and I am blessed because Jesus died for me!

God is with me like a mighty terrible one:

> Jeremiah 20:11-13
>
> [11] But the LORD is with me as a mighty terrible one: therefore my persecutors shall stumble, and they shall not prevail: they shall be greatly ashamed; for they shall not prosper: their everlasting confusion shall never be forgotten.
>
> [12] But, O LORD of hosts, that triest the righteous, and seest the reins and the heart, let me see thy vengeance on them: for unto thee have I opened my cause.
>
> [13] Sing unto the LORD, praise ye the LORD: for he hath delivered the soul of the poor from the hand of evildoers.

We can read in the Bible and understand how God defeats all evildoers. **His Word is powerful and never returns void**.

God is forming a special people. For this reason, He allows us to face opposition so that we may learn how to use the authority and power He has given us to fight. **Luke 10:19**

Each time we face a battle, we are given the opportunity to fight with His power; and each time we have victory, we rise to a new level, a higher level. We become stronger, wiser, and we are formed into the image of God when we place our trust and faith in Him and His Word.

Isaiah 55:10-11

[10] For as the rain cometh down, and the snow from heaven, and returneth not thither, but watereth the earth, and maketh it bring forth and bud, that it may give seed to the sower, and bread to the eater:

[11] So shall my word be that goeth forth out of my mouth: it **shall not return unto me void**, but it shall accomplish that which I please, and it shall prosper in the thing whereto I sent it.

In order to succeed in life, to live a life with purpose, to be able to face difficulties and battles, we must meditate in the Word of God, each day. That is the way to become nourished and fortified! We read, study and learn from what the Bible says and we are guaranteed victory!

Psalm 1:1-3

Blessed is the man that walketh not in the counsel of the ungodly, nor standeth in the way of sinners, nor sitteth in the seat of the scornful.

[2] But his delight is in the law of the LORD; and in his law doth he meditate day and night.

[3] And he shall be like a tree planted by the rivers of water, that bringeth forth his fruit in his season; his leaf also shall not wither; and whatsoever he doeth shall prosper.

Your victory is written in the Word of God.

Your prosperity is found when you meditate in the perfect law of God (His law is His Word), and when you walk (walk is to live) according to His Word (Live in obedience to His Word).

Psalm 23:4
⁴Yea, though I walk through the valley of the shadow of death, I will fear no evil: for thou art with me; thy rod and thy staff they comfort me.

It is when we are walking through our valley, it is when we are facing trials, tribulations, difficulty, sickness, hurt, deception, it is in that valley that we learn how to battle all evildoers; against all evil spirits; against all strange voices.

Isaiah 35:9-10
⁹No lion shall be there, nor any ravenous beast shall go up thereon, it shall not be found there; but the redeemed shall walk there:
¹⁰And the ransomed of the LORD shall return, and come to Zion with songs and everlasting joy upon their heads: they shall obtain joy and gladness, and sorrow and sighing shall flee away.

In life, we encounter lions and ravenous beasts. But, as we learn to meditate in God's Word, we gain the ability to identify the enemy. We also gain strength to walk victoriously by using the power of His Word. How do we use it? Well, we read it, we believe it, and then we speak it. It doesn't matter what we see, we just believe what the Word of God says and we walk in it, by faith, by confessing it.

The promises of God in His Word are for the redeemed. If you have accepted Jesus as your savior, each promise of God is for you.

The beasts cannot face you and defeat you. They will face you but they will be defeated. You are protected by the power of God.

God wants to pour everlasting joy upon your head; God enjoys to see you with gladness.

It is not God's will to see us in affliction, with sadness, and weeping. God wants to see us rejoicing and celebrating in His presence.

Psalm 57:2-4

[2] I will cry unto God most high; unto God that performeth all things for me.

[3] He shall send from heaven, and save me from the reproach of him that would swallow me up. Selah. God shall send forth his mercy and his truth.

[4] My soul is among lions: and I lie even among them that are set on fire, even the sons of men, whose teeth are spears and arrows, and their tongue a sharp sword.

Verse 4 above reveals our state of being when we walk through the valley and the plan of the enemy is to destroy us. For this reason, we are overwhelmed with fear, confusion, depression, and other attacks. However, the Word of God is clear, it is true, it is what God says! The question is: What are we going to do when fear arrives or when the attacks arrive? The decision is ours. Our decision will lead us to defeat or victory. Why not choose victory? We need to place our trust in the Lord and His Word. Accept the counsel of the Lord and be victorious.

Well, I'm almost done with my journey and my enemies had to flee. They all left because they were attacked with a sharp sword, they were faced with the Word of God!

Psalm 23:5

[5] Thou preparest a table before me in the presence of mine enemies: thou anointest my head with oil; my cup runneth over.

You might not know who your enemies are. But when you are walking with God, when you are meditating in His Word, obeying His counsel, and when you live in a manner that pleases God, your enemies will see how God defends you and blesses you. They get to witness God in your life!

John 10:10

[10] The thief cometh not, but for to steal, and to kill, and to destroy: I am come that they might have life, and that they might have it more abundantly.

A thief (your enemy) may identify himself as friendly, with kind words, but his plan is to steal, to kill, to destroy you and your loved ones.

The plan of the enemy is to rob you of everything. The thief wants to rob your peace, joy, business, finances, children, marriage, health, and salvation.

The thief will try to destroy all the good things God has for you or all the good things that God has given you. He will try to rob you of good ideas, and he will try to rob you of a clear mind. The enemy will try to rob you of a kind spirit. The enemy (*Satan and his army of demons/The Kingdom of Darkness*) comes near you to rob you in order to destroy you. He will do whatever he can to weaken you. That is why it is so important to be alert! It is important to study the Word of God, treasure it and put it into practice! It is your strength! It is your shield! It is your sword! It is your victory!

The enemy enjoys involving you in anything that is not approved by God. The enemy wants you to lose out because he does not want you to receive salvation. Therefore, be cautious not to fall into his trap of walking in a life of sin.

It is in such a deceitful manner that Satan will rob you of opportunities to be successful. He will send discouragement, confusion, bitterness, and whatever foul spirit to defeat God's purpose and plan to prosper you. That is why we need to have a leader. We need God to lead us, to teach us, to direct us. God gives us security, and he provides all that we need.

John 10:11

[11] I am the good shepherd: the good shepherd giveth his life for the sheep.

Jesus is always on time! He offers a table of love, mercy, peace, joy, and hope. He pours everlasting joy over us, He left his presence: the Holy

Spirit, to guide us in His truth. He guides us with understanding in all situations.

God fills us with a joy that strengthens us; a joy that cannot be explained:

Nehemiah 8:9-10
⁹ And Nehemiah, which is the Tirshatha, and Ezra the priest the scribe, and the Levites that taught the people, said unto all the people, This day is holy unto the LORD your God; mourn not, nor weep. For all the people wept, when they heard the words of the law.
¹⁰ Then he said unto them, Go your way, eat the fat, and drink the sweet, and send portions unto them for whom nothing is prepared: for this day is holy unto our LORD: neither be ye sorry; for the joy of the LORD is your strength.

The people were in a distraught state because their enemies had destroyed the walls of their city; they were oppressed by their adversaries; but God heard their weeping and their cry and sent help to rebuild the walls. When the work was done, the Lord sent them a message that He was their joy.

The Word of God brings comfort when we are oppressed by our enemies; and the Word reminds us that He sees all that is done against us, to harm us; and that He hears our prayers, He sends help and allows the enemy to see that He, the Lord himself, is with us.

Romans 8:37-39
³⁷ Nay, in all these things we are more than conquerors through him that loved us.
³⁸ For I am persuaded, that neither death, nor life, nor angels, nor principalities, nor powers, nor things present, nor things to come,
³⁹ Nor height, nor depth, nor any other creature, shall be able to separate us from the love of God, which is in Christ Jesus our Lord.

Our journey is one of formation. We are in a constant state of being trained. With each lesson, we are molded; we grow; we become better prepared for the following level. **Romans 8:37-39** should be declared by us constantly. God's goal is to form us so that we are moved into position to fulfill His divine purpose in our lives. Whatever we are called for, whatever our purpose in life is, let us understand that all things, whatever happens to us, whether good or not so good, all things work together for our good.

Once we understand what we are called for, and once we are mature in His Word, we then understand and are able to perceive how the enemy tries so hard to stop us; to deviate us from God's divine purpose and plans.

Throughout life, the enemy will try to excel, to destroy us. For this reason, we are to ask God for wisdom, guidance and understanding.

Once we understand that God loves us, that He has great and beautiful plans for us and then we decide to accept Jesus as our savior, it is then that we can walk with God's wisdom and understanding. He pours His favor and grace over us, which empowers us. We then no longer walk alone without perfect direction; we then walk with the company of the Holy Spirit that leads us and guides us. That is when we will know the goodness of God's truth and that with Him and only through Him we are more than conquerors.

Psalm 23:6
⁶ Surely goodness and mercy shall follow me all the days of my life: and I will dwell in the house of the LORD forever.

Everything that God brings to us is good!

Jeremiah 29:11
¹¹ For I know the thoughts that I think toward you, saith the LORD, thoughts of peace, and not of evil, to give you an expected end.

God's plans for you are the best!
God is merciful:

Psalm 136:1
O give thanks unto the LORD; for he is good: for his mercy endureth forever.

When we talk about our journey, we are referring to life; when we talk about a valley, we are talking about a difficult time - a time of desperation - a time of hurt - a time of darkness; and we go through different "seasons" throughout our journey as well. We experience seasons of sowing; seasons of reaping; seasons of silence and seasons of noise; seasons of sorrow and seasons of celebration. Often times we want to rush through our valley but we can't.

We ought to be obedient to God's word and we will see how the enemy gets uncomfortable. Yes, the Devil gets uncomfortable when you are going through a trial and you are still singing; when you are sick and you are still worshiping God; he gets annoyed! But, just trust God in the middle of whatever storm you go through and He will bring you to the mountaintop!

Let us accept the counsel of the Lord, the instructions of God's word:

Ephesians 6:10-17
[10] Finally, my brethren, be strong in the Lord, and in the power of his might.
[11] Put on the whole armour of God, that ye may be able to stand against the wiles of the devil.
[12] For we wrestle not against flesh and blood, but against principalities, against powers, against the rulers of the darkness of this world, against spiritual wickedness in high places.
[13] Wherefore take unto you the whole armour of God, that ye may be able to withstand in the evil day, and having done all, to stand.
[14] Stand therefore, having your loins girt about with truth, and having on the breastplate of righteousness;
[15] And your feet shod with the preparation of the gospel of peace;
[16] Above all, taking the shield of faith, wherewith ye shall be able to quench all the fiery darts of the wicked.

[17] And take the helmet of salvation, and the sword of the Spirit, which is the word of God.

This portion of God's Word mentions the dress of the believer. We ought to be dressed to confront our adversaries; to confront wickedness; to face difficulty; and to battle unexpected warfare. Once again, the Word of God is specific and teaches us to be dressed, to be prepared, and how to be sure of our victory.

Psalm 27:1-2

The LORD is my light and my salvation; whom shall I fear? the LORD is the strength of my life; of whom shall I be afraid?

[2] When the wicked, even mine enemies and my foes, came upon me to eat up my flesh, they stumbled and fell.

It is time for victory over your enemies! It is time to see the power of the Word of God in our lives.

I now understand that we cannot place our trust on ourselves, or on any man; we place our trust in God. We must ask God for discernment and to give us revelation of what He wants to reveal to us.

And the three of us, all jump for joy as we noticed that after talking and walking for a short distance- we have reached the beautiful mountaintop! We begin to laugh, to hug, and we hold hands and look up to the heavens; we begin to give thanks to the one that gave us strength while we were struggling in the valley and to the only who deserves worship for bringing us up to the mountaintop! What a great and rewarding feeling to be able to help others!

Thank God for his goodness, his mercy and faithfulness for when I cried out, he heard me and he answered me.

As long as we set our eyes on God; as long as we are focused on what God's Word teaches us; as long as we are obedient to the Word of God; as long as we keep hold to God's truths and promises, we will succeed and we will see victory!

There is one guarantee in life that you can count on: God will never fail you!

The secret to receiving God's help is *to just talk to Him!*
Invite Jesus into your heart;
Ask God for forgiveness;
Ask God for mercy;
Ask God to dress you with his armor;
Ask God's goodness to follow you;
Ask God to send His Holy Spirit to be your companion;
As Jesus to live in your heart;
Your victory is promised!
Your blessings are countless!

To you, reading this book, I invite you to make a decision today to accept Jesus as your Lord and Savior. You can start by reading aloud the following prayer of salvation:

> Jesus, I know that you died upon a cross for me!
> You rose again to save the lost and I now ask
> you to forgive me for all of my sin.
> I ask you to be my Savior, Lord and Friend.
> Make me a new creation and change my life.
> Please help me to live for you.
> *Amen*

If you have received the Lord Jesus in your heart as your Savior, you are now born again, a new creation!

You have new companions: God's presence and His Holy Spirit are with you always. God's goodness and mercy follow you always. Your valley is no longer dark for God has filled you with his light! You are ready to receive his blessings!

Proverbs 3:5
5 Trust in the LORD with all thine heart; and lean not unto thine own understanding.

Trust the Lord and you will be blessed!

CONFUSION
Inability to engage in orderly thought; inability to distinguish or make decisions; lack of understanding, a situation of panic, a breakdown of order, unsureness

DEPRESSION
An illness that involves the body, mood and thoughts and that affects the way a person eats, sleeps and feels

(while writing this book, I was deeply hurt to hear a news report of a young lady that talked about "her friend DEPRESSION visiting her". She eventually ended her life. This is the way the enemy brings destruction...)

SADNESS
A mental state of altered mood, despair, discouragement, lowering of functional activity

DISCOURAGEMENT
The act of trying to make someone not want to do something; intimidate, frighten, dishearten by expressing disapproval

FEAR
Paralyzes, excessive anxiety for no logical reason, obsessive-compulsive disorder, makes us unproductive, makes us ineffective

ANGUISH
Severe physical or emotional pain or distress.

GUILT
Unhappy feeling because you think you have done something wrong or you have done something wrong; feelings of regret, tension, remorse, culpable

TEMPTATION
The desire to do something wrong or unwise

PRIDE
An unreasonable feeling of being superior as to beauty, rank, talent; superiority feeling derived from one's own achievements; self-admiration

ENVY
Being discontent or resentful because of someone else's achievements, possessions or success; covetousness; jealousy

VANITY
Excessive admiration of one's own achievements or appearance; conceit

BITTERNESS
Showing feelings of strong hatred, anger, resentment

LOW-SELF ESTEEM
General feeling of insignificance; lack of importance; feel inadequate

CONFRONTATION
A hostile meeting between opposing parties; battle;

CURSE
Invoke misfortune, to afflict, to insult, to invoke a supernatural power to punish

A man finds a young girl sitting, crying, in The Valley.

Psalm 23:4-6

4 *Yea, though I walk through the valley of the shadow of death, I will fear no evil: for thou art with me; thy rod and thy staff they comfort me.*
5 *Thou preparest a table before me in the presence of mine enemies: thou anointest my head with oil; my cup runneth over.*
6 *Surely goodness and mercy shall follow me all the days of my life: and I will dwell in the house of the* LORD *for ever.*

The Prayer of Salvation

Jesus, I know that you died upon a cross for me!
You rose again to save the lost and I now ask
you to forgive me for all of my sin.
I ask you to be my Savior, Lord and Friend.
Make me a new creation and change my life.
Please help me to live for you.
Amen

If you would like prayer, feel free to send an email:
Psalms23TheValley@gmail.com

Printed in the United States
By Bookmasters